Fantastic! My new 'go to' book about behaviour. Tamsin's wealth of experience, knowledge and writing style has enabled her to find the perfect balance between theory/research/practical examples to create a really clear companion to reflective practice.

Her refreshing and realistic approach recognises the challenges for practitioners and the complex influences on behaviour for the children in their care. As we know there is no quick fix for 'behaviour' that we find challenging. But increasing our emotional, mental health and trauma awareness enables us to use a proactive, nurturing, loving pedagogy to develop an ethos that will give adults and children the 'best possible chance' of feeling listened to and understood. As Tamsin says and demonstrates in her practical suggestions, by 'responding mindfully rather than reacting emotionally' we can improve our practice and each child's experience incrementally day by day.

Dr Kay Mathieson, *international speaker, author and independent early years consultant*

Supporting Behaviour and Emotions in the Early Years

Have you ever wondered why children behave the way they do or why they can become overwhelmed with emotions so quickly? This practical resource has been created to help educators effectively support their children's behaviour and better understand their emotions.

The book focuses on the idea that all behaviour is a form of communication and explores central areas such as self-regulation and attachment, offering strategies that can be used to support challenging behaviour. Each chapter includes examples of practice, reflective questions and an activity for the reader to help consolidate their learning and encourage them to become 'behaviour detectives'.

Key topics discussed include:

* Attachment theory, adverse childhood experiences and the importance of feeling safe and secure in the home and setting.
* Characteristics of children during conflict situations or moments of challenging behaviour.
* Developmentally appropriate expectations for children, and why it is vital that expectations are realistic.
* Emotion coaching and the significance of acknowledging and validating feelings.
* Linking behaviour with schematic play.

Written from first-hand experience and filled with practical advice as well as recommendations for further reading and resources, *Supporting Behaviour and Emotions in the Early Years* is an essential read for early years educators.

Tamsin Grimmer is the early years director of Linden Learning and teaches on the Primary and Early Years Initial Teacher Training PGCE Programmes at Bath Spa University. She has a wealth of experience and has written several books supporting early years teachers and educators. Tamsin is passionate about young children's learning and development and is fascinated by how very young children think. She believes that all children deserve educators who are inspiring, dynamic, reflective and loving. She has coined the phrase 'loving pedagogy' and has a keen interest in schematic play, promoting positive behaviour and supporting children's emotional development.

Little Minds Matter:

Promoting Social and Emotional Wellbeing in the Early Years

Series Advisor: Sonia Mainstone-Cotton

The *Little Minds Matter* series promotes best practice for integrating social and emotional health and wellbeing into the early years setting. It introduces practitioners to a wealth of activities and resources to support them in each key area: from providing access to ideas for unstructured, imaginative outdoor play; activities to create a sense of belonging and form positive identities; and, importantly, strategies to encourage early years professionals to create a workplace that positively contributes to their own wellbeing, as well as the quality of their provision. The *Little Minds Matter* series ensures that practitioners have the tools they need to support every child.

Outdoor Play for Healthy Little Minds
Practical Ideas to Promote Children's Wellbeing in the Early Years
Sarah Watkins

Supporting the Wellbeing of Children with SEND
Essential Ideas for Early Years Educators
Kerry Payne

Supporting Behaviour and Emotions in the Early Years
Strategies and Ideas for Early Years Educators
Tamsin Grimmer

Supporting Behaviour and Emotions in the Early Years

Strategies and Ideas for Early Years Educators

Tamsin Grimmer

Routledge
Taylor & Francis Group

LONDON AND NEW YORK

Cover image: The picture on the cover was drawn by Bea who has just started school and is 4 years old. It shows her teacher holding hands with Bea and her friends to make her friend feel better after falling over.

First published 2022
by Routledge
4 Park Square, Milton Park, Abingdon, Oxon OX14 4RN

and by Routledge
605 Third Avenue, New York, NY 10158

Routledge is an imprint of the Taylor & Francis Group, an informa business

© 2022 Tamsin Grimmer

The right of Tamsin Grimmer to be identified as author of this work has been asserted in accordance with sections 77 and 78 of the Copyright, Designs and Patents Act 1988.

British Library Cataloguing-in-Publication Data
A catalogue record for this book is available from the British Library

Library of Congress Cataloging-in-Publication Data
Names: Grimmer, Tamsin, author.
Title: Supporting behaviour and emotions in the early years: strategies and ideas for early years educators / Tamsin Grimmer.
Description: Abingdon, Oxon; New York, NY: Routledge, 2022. | Series: Little minds matter | Includes bibliographical references and index.
Identifiers: LCCN 2021048124 (print) | LCCN 2021048125 (ebook) | ISBN 9780367684273 (hardback) | ISBN 9780367684259 (paperback) | ISBN 9781003137474 (ebook)
Subjects: LCSH: Early childhood education–Psychological aspects. | Behavior modification. | Emotions in children.
Classification: LCC LB1060.2 .G75 2022 (print) | LCC LB1060.2 (ebook) | DDC 370.15/28–dc23/eng/20211103
LC record available at https://lccn.loc.gov/2021048124
LC ebook record available at https://lccn.loc.gov/2021048125

ISBN: 978-0-367-68427-3 (hbk)
ISBN: 978-0-367-68425-9 (pbk)
ISBN: 978-1-003-13747-4 (ebk)

DOI: 10.4324/9781003137474

Typeset in Optima
by Deanta Global Publishing Services, Chennai, India

Access the Support Material: www.routledge.com/9780367684259

This book is dedicated to my three daughters who have taught me all about behaviour as communication and how it links to our emotions. I love you.

Contents

Acknowledgements

Firstly may I thank Sonia Mainstone-Cotton for her continued support and the team at Routledge for encouraging me to write this book. I have really loved writing it because it brings together my thinking around behaviour, loving pedagogy and schemas so nicely. It would not have been possible without the lovely anecdotes and case studies from so many wonderful educators – thank you. I particularly want to thank:

Annika Hart, Hornbeams Preschool
Candice McIntyre and Charlotte Adcock, Westview Day Nursery
Chloe Webster, Pebbles Childminding
Dena Moore, Widcombe Acorns Preschool
Emma Burt and Chloe Jackman, St Catherine's Pre-School
Emma Stamford, Roseacre Primary Academy
Helene Wells, Childminder
Jenna Jefferies and Amy Hunter, Charlton Nursery
Jess Gosling, International School Early Years Teacher
Julie Reed, Norfolk House Nursery
Katherine Bate, Cinnamon Brow Primary School and Nursery
Marlis Juerging-Coles, St John's Preschool
Megan Bowkett, Mulberry Bush Preschool
Naomi de Chastelain, Hemington Primary School
Rachel Tomlinson, Barrowford Primary School
Bath Spa Teachers including Annika Hart, Gemma Rowlands, Ruby Moxley, Jennie Holloway, Candice McIntyre, Jenna Jefferies

Lastly, but most importantly, my family deserves thanks for allowing me the time to write and providing me with so much inspiration over the years. Mum, for her patient proofreading of my chapters, and my husband Richard, for his ongoing love and belief in me.

Foreword

This latest book in the Little Minds Matter series looks at how we can support behaviours and emotions, enabling children to communicate their feelings through positive behaviour. I believe this is an essential book for us to have in our series; it is so easy to get caught up in the deficit lens of behaviour. Tamsin challenges this view and offers many ideas, suggestions and insights into behaviour, recognising how behaviour is the primary way a child communicates to us, underpinning our understanding of behaviour through emotion language and insight into the child's world.

Tamsin weaves through many ideas and suggestions based on her own and others' experiences. Throughout the book, we hear the voices of a wide variety of practitioners sharing their examples; this enables us all to find models similar to the situation we are in, making this book relevant across early years sectors and for parents.

This book covers a comprehensive introduction to ideas around supporting behaviours and emotions. If this is a new area to you, the book will give you an excellent oversight into supporting the child and will encourage you to reflect on what might be happening for the child. If this is a familiar subject for you, you will find many ideas and suggestions to assist you in furthering your toolbox of ideas. In Chapter 3, Tamsin focuses on Theory of Mind; sometimes writing on this can be baffling, however, Tamsin explains Theory of Mind in an accessible way. I found this chapter so helpful, and I will be sharing it with staff to help me explain Theory of Mind. Chapter 5 is titled 'Becoming a behaviour detective'. I love this description, and it is one I will be adopting; this chapter is fantastic at helping us to think about what the child is communicating through their behaviour and offers practical ideas and suggestions.

The key message is about the importance of the relationship between adult and child and our need to love the child – an important message for us all to adopt. I hope you enjoy reading this latest book in our series, and I am sure you will take away ideas to try.

Sonia Mainstone-Cotton
Series Advisor
September 2021

 # Introduction

Children can behave in ways that we sometimes find difficult to cope with or understand. I believe that if we better understand children's social, emotional and mental health (SEMH) needs we will respond more appropriately to them and this, in turn, will help us to support our children more effectively. Some children with SEMH needs will have special educational needs or learn differently, whilst others may not have any diagnosed additional needs. We all have times when our emotions impact our behaviour and we need additional support, so supporting children's SEMH is part of being an inclusive practitioner.

This book is all about supporting behaviour and emotions and I hope will help adults to explore their role when responding to children. I have chosen not to talk in terms of adults controlling children's behaviour or behaviour management. Instead I will focus on understanding children's behaviour and responding appropriately. The reason why I will avoid terms like control and manage from the adult's perspective is because my approach is not about how adults can *make* children behave in a certain way, but rather how we can support children when they have these big feelings and emotions that might manifest in behaviour that adults find challenging.

In addition, although I may use terms like challenging, I want to explain that it is not the children who are challenging but the behaviour, and the challenge is for us as educators to better understand them. So we need to respond proactively rather than reactively to our children. We must avoid thinking about the children themselves as being the problem, for example 'the biter, the hitter, the tricky one…' Instead we must see it as an opportunity for us to hone our skills in problem

DOI: 10.4324/9781003137474-1

solving, conflict resolution and emotion coaching to help the children when they feel like biting or hitting or feeling dysregulated. It is my belief that young children do not want to misbehave – they want to be loved, understood and accepted for who they are.

Behaviour is communication

A main thread running through this book views all behaviour as communication. So everything that a child says and does and the emotions that they feel all communicate something to us as their educators, parents or carers. All we have to do is work out what they are communicating. Although this sounds easy, it is not always as straightforward as we might hope.

Let's first of all think about communication and where this stems from. As babies we are born already social beings, eager to communicate with others. We seek out interaction, connection and develop attachments to those who are important to us. From our earliest days we need to learn how to understand what other people say and then develop our language and communication skills. Despite the popular belief that language learning is innate, it actually relies upon growing up in a language-rich environment surrounded by people eager to communicate with us.

There are a number of language and communication skills to learn too. For example, we need to learn to use our voice, words, gestures and body in order to communicate, we need to actively listen to others and we need to learn the serve and return of interaction. In addition to this, we will also need to learn how to use words properly, speak clearly and eventually learn the components of language (phonology, semantics, grammar and pragmatics). It's not an easy task! Communication is all about connection and seeing behaviour as another form of communication reminds us of the importance of connecting with our children.

Thinking about what children are communicating helps us to investigate the root causes of behaviour and then we can try to address the underlying needs. One analogy that I find helpful is to think of the behaviour we see as just the tip of an iceberg. We can all picture an iceberg with a small amount of ice above the water line and lots more ice underneath. If the seen behaviour is only the tip it reminds us that underneath what we see there is a lot more going on. Chapter 2 explores some reasons why children behave the way they do and Chapter 5 invites us to use this iceberg analogy to unpick the behaviour of our own children.

Let's think about this in practice. We might see a child behaving in a way that displeases us, perhaps they are lashing out and hitting someone. This is the *seen* behaviour but actually the child is really communicating something else. They might be saying that they are very angry or that they are feeling really overwhelmed with emotion right now. Or perhaps they are communicating that they really wanted a particular toy and have not yet developed the necessary language to ask for it. Our role is to try to unpick what is underneath the surface. We need to become behaviour detectives and work out what they are communicating with us. Chapter 5 explores this more fully.

Our emotions underpin our behaviour

Thinking about behaviour as communication is helpful because it can encourage us to also consider the emotions that underpin our behaviour. The way we feel is usually displayed through our actions, what we say and how we react. For example, if a young child is upset, they might cry and need comfort and if they are angry they might want to lash out and hit. We behave in specific ways because we feel a certain way – the emotion is underpinning the behaviour.

If we want to support children with their behaviour and respond appropriately to them, we need to unpick, understand and support their emotions. It is vitally important to acknowledge and validate children's feelings and using an emotion coaching approach can help. Chapter 4 focuses on this. Exploring behaviour and emotions together gives educators the opportunity to fully understand the emotional needs of their children and the impact that this has on behaviour. It is my hope that this book will empower educators as they support children's behaviour and emotions and, in turn, empower children as they are better understood and responded to appropriately.

Outline of book

This book is divided into chapters which all consider a different aspect relating to children's behaviour and emotions within the broader umbrella of

SEMH. There is an activity towards the end of each chapter which encourages the reader to put into practice the ideas from the chapter and there are a few questions listed designed to encourage reflection on practice. Each chapter also includes case studies which I am sharing to illustrate the points made and demonstrate how some settings support children's behaviour and emotions in practice. I use the term setting in its broadest sense to include preschool, nursery, childminding setting, school, breakfast or after school club, in fact, any provider who looks after early years children. I use the term educator to mean any adult who is working directly with children in a setting, regardless of their level of qualification or experience. When I refer to parents I am also including other adults, in addition to birth parents, who are the main carers for a child, for example foster carers, grandparents or step-parents.

The first chapter will link children's behaviour to attachment theory, adverse childhood experiences (ACES) and the importance of feeling safe and secure in our home and setting. It will explain that there are some factors that inhibit children from learning or prevent them from feeling safe and secure, and the key message will be that, although some issues can feel out of our control, we need to always respond to the child and family with sensitivity and empathy.

The second chapter will explore why children behave the way they do, for example, unmet basic needs, frustration at not being understood or sharing objects. It will remind readers about our emotional responses, e.g. freeze, fight or flight, and how we are unable to think when our emotions take over.

Chapter 3 explores developmentally appropriate expectations for our children and why it is vital that our expectations are realistic. It unpicks concepts like sharing in a developmentally appropriate way and shares age-stage expectations relating to behaviour in line with typical development, whilst explaining that emotionally many children will not work at this typical level. It also considers how we can better understand individual differences such as age, gender, temperament or family values.

The fourth chapter explains the importance of validating feelings and considers how we can use an emotion coaching response style. The key message is that all emotions and feelings are acceptable but not all behaviour. It will share useful phrases to employ with children and examples of how to use an emotion coaching approach in practice, sharing strategies like the problem-solving technique for conflict resolution.

Chapter 5 will share the importance of observation and getting to know our children really well. It will suggest that practitioners are very good at finding out children's interests but may not have considered this from an emotional perspective. For example, what makes a child calm, angry or upset? Is there anything they feel anxious or frightened about? It is important as practitioners to get to know our children really well emotionally. It is as if we are behaviour detectives – trying to work out what the children are communicating, how they feel and what they think through careful observation, listening to them and talking with parents and carers.

Chapter 6 explores several specific strategies to support children when they behave in challenging ways, when distraction or ignoring can successfully work, and what to do if a child has a tantrum. Our response should be non-judgemental and there is no sliding scale of poor behaviour, instead there are children who are feeling big feelings and have not yet learned how to cope with them.

The seventh chapter will explore self-regulation and reframe the idea of 'managing behaviour' into 'supporting' children to develop self-regulation. The key message will be that through becoming a co-regulator we can help children to develop self-regulation. It will consider how we can de-escalate situations through the way we respond sensitively, acknowledging feelings and by being non-judgemental and how we can support children to manage their big emotions.

Chapter 8 tries to shed light on the sometimes confusing or intriguing ways that children behave which are difficult for us to fathom, for example always throwing things, plugging the sink with tissue paper or unravelling the toilet roll. These behaviours can be described as schematic, when children engage in repetitive behaviours or actions. Reinterpreting them in the light of schemas helps us to respond more appropriately by finding the children alternative experiences which tap into their fascination or schema.

Chapter 9 thinks about how our policy and practice should be underpinned by our ethos when working with young children. It considers the important role that parents play as the child's first educator and the importance and benefits of collaboration. It will also think about the other professionals that educators may need to liaise with. This chapter will also briefly explain why using behaviour charts such as a traffic light system can have a very negative impact on children's wellbeing and emotional development.

The conclusion sums up the key points from the book and offers a few more ideas of how we can support children's behaviour and emotions moving forward. It also includes several more questions for reflection which will help the reader to review their practice in the light of the book.

Feeling safe and secure

This chapter will link children's behaviour to attachment theory, adverse childhood experiences and the importance of feeling safe and secure in our home and setting. It will explain that there are some factors that inhibit children from learning or prevent them from feeling safe and secure and early childhood educators have a key role to play in helping and supporting children.

Introduction

Before we can begin to support children with their behaviour, we need to consider the many factors that may inhibit children and prevent them from feeling OK in the first place. Chapter 2 explores several reasons why children might behave the way they do and suggests that children's basic needs should be met. One of these needs is the feeling of safety and security. It is this feeling that underpins our social, emotional and mental health.

If I were to go on a bus journey and felt the driver was driving erratically and dangerously, I would want to get off the bus as soon as possible. Feeling unsafe is not a good way to feel. If I were to snuggle up on our sofa at home with a blanket over me and watch my favourite film I would feel really safe and secure. For me, home is a safe haven and secure base where I can relax and just be, and having time at home enables me to face the big wide world! It is vital that children feel safe and secure in their homes, but also in our settings – if they do not, they will not be ready to learn.

DOI: 10.4324/9781003137474-2

Attachment theory

There are obvious links here with attachment theory. Bowlby, the founder of attachment theory, explains that 'All of us, from cradle to grave, are happiest when life is organized as a series of excursions, long or short, from the secure base provided by our attachment figure(s)' (Bowlby, 1988, p. 62). Attachments impact on our whole lives one way or another; just as I feel that home is a safe place for me, we need our children to see our settings in this way.

The foundation for children's social, emotional and mental health begins with the first attachments they make with their primary caregivers. The nature of this relationship determines their ability to form relationships with others and research has shown that secure attachments are linked with higher academic achievement, better self-regulatory skills and an ability to function socially (Bergin & Bergin, 2009). Holmes describes attachment literally as a spatial theory because we feel safe, secure and comforted when we are in the presence of the people we have the strongest attachments with (2014). Attachment theory proposes that having a secure attachment contributes to feelings of safety and security and the opposite of this is having an insecure attachment, when we are not confident that we are safe and secure.

Proximity seeking

Generally speaking attachment theory suggests that children may initially want to remain in close proximity to their main caregiver. We may see this when a child is visiting our setting for the first time and they may initially hide behind their parent's legs, appear shy and not want to leave their parent's side or when a toddler follows their main carer around, even into the bathroom! Initially this strong bond is usually with their mother, although over time additional attachments become just as important. We may also find children displaying strong attachments to certain toys or objects. These are very important to the child and we should be wary of removing them. Sometimes they can become instrumental in helping to soothe or settle a child and can be used as a transitional object that goes between home and setting like a constant friend. We do this too as adults, when we keep a memento of a friend or loved one to help us remember them.

TRANSITIONAL OBJECTS – A CHILDMINDER'S PERSPECTIVE

We are firm believers in and advocates for transitional objects and understand the vast importance these objects have on children of all ages during times of change and transition, whether into a new setting or even into a new room within their current setting. These objects are of huge importance to the child and, whilst we may not fully understand the child's heightened attachment to a particular item, its value should not be overlooked.

We have experienced a number of different transitional objects within our setting but one in particular is the use of a small comforter blanket attached to a teddy. When Maisie started with us aged 1 year old, this object was pivotal in her successful transition into the setting and during her settling-in periods she liked to have the object nearby and often sucked on its label for comfort.

As Maisie's confidence grew, her reliance on her transitional object subsided significantly and we quickly developed from having the object on her person at all times to only seeing it at drop-offs and nap times, with Maisie happily putting it in her bag once she'd arrived.

Maisie, now aged 3, still has this transitional object, but it stays in the bag throughout her full day session, however she knows the object is in the bag if she needs it and that is more than enough for her to feel confident.

We have experienced varying degrees of reliance on the object, for example upon Maisie's return to the setting after lockdown, but again, in her own time, her reliance on the object dwindled and we moved back to having the object in the bag and out for nap times, before finally resorting back to it staying firmly in the bag throughout her session.

We believe that as long as the object is not hindering the child's ability to participate within the setting and within a group, then it is only a supportive tool that allows the child to feel confident, settle and thus engage significantly more with their experiences within the setting. Forcing the child to give up the object or to take it away against the child's will is much more traumatic for them and will only further hinder their confidence.

Safe haven

When children have a strong attachment to an adult they will want to remain close to that adult; however, once they become more comfortable and confident in their surrounding environment, they will begin to go off and explore. If at any point they feel worried, anxious or frightened, they will immediately return to their attachment figure for protection and comfort. So thinking about the example of a child visiting our setting with their parent, if we linger in a room for a while, their parent may suggest they go and play, which they happily do. However, if there was a loud noise or a stranger entered the room, the child would most likely return to their parent's side again to be reassured. We also see this if a child falls and hurts themselves, they often return to their caregiver for comfort, or if they are scared, they will seek the close proximity of their caregiver again. We need to be aware that this is typical behaviour and ensure we are available to our children, so that when they seek us we can be found.

Secure base

Ainsworth coined the phrase 'secure base' and discusses how children use their mother in this way, feeling comfortable enough knowing she is there to leave her and explore their surrounding environment (Ainsworth et al., 1978). We see this in attachment relationships in our settings when children feel at ease and comfortable, secure in their knowledge that they are loved and cared for by us and they are keen to engage in our provision. If a child does not feel secure, they would not feel able to explore and investigate within our settings. We need our children to use our settings as secure bases from which to explore the world.

Separation anxiety

We have all come across children who find it difficult to separate from their parent in the morning when they are dropped off at our settings. Many children will struggle with being apart from their main carer and this is a typical part of a secure attachment. If we try to prise a child from their parent's arms, we may experience clinging, screaming and even violent behaviour. If we think about it, this should not be surprising, because we are trying to take a child away from their source of safety, security and comfort. In doing so we are dysregulating the child and making them feel under threat. Chapter 2 explores our body and brain's response to this and Chapter 4 reiterates the importance of a response that acknowledges and validates feelings. When a child has separation anxiety we must respond sensitively and empathetically. Using an emotion coaching approach can help, gently talking to the child and explaining how we think they are feeling and why; for example, 'You're feeling sad because mummy had to go to work. She's coming back later. While we wait for her, let's go and play…'

If we anticipate that a child may have separation anxiety, we can actively plan for it, by ensuring their favourite resources are accessible, and perhaps their key person or the adult they have the strongest bond with is on hand. We can also work closely with parents to try to make the handover as fast as practically possible because sometimes a prolonged goodbye can make the separation harder. Sticking to the same routine can really help too. One child I looked after used to want to go home straight after lunch, so I let him wear his coat whilst playing in the afternoon, ensuring he didn't overheat! This reassured him that he was ready to leave, even though I knew he still had another couple of hours left. Other ideas which can help with separation anxiety and attachment issues include:

- Use a visual timetable which clearly shows hometime.
- Have a consistent daily routine and handover routine.
- Create a photo tag or keyring with a picture of both parent and child which can be attached to the child's bag or coat.
- Provide the child with a small photo of their family to keep in their pocket.
- Display photos of the children's families on the wall so that we can look at them at any time during the session.
- Ask the parent to draw a heart on their wrist and another on their child's wrist. When the child feels upset they can press the heart and feel the love.
- Create or purchase 'bestie' necklaces which come in two halves, one for the parent and one for the child.

- Ask the parent to provide a hankie with a dab of perfume or aftershave on so that it will smell familiar to the child.
- Encourage the parent to include a little note in their child's lunchbox with a heart or message for the child.
- Use stories such as *The Invisible String* by Patrice Karst (2018) and *Owl Babies* by Martin Waddell (1992) to talk about being apart from the people we love.

SEPARATION ANXIETY – A PARENT'S PERSPECTIVE

When my daughter was younger she used to find it difficult to separate from me. I talked to her teacher about how best to support her. We decided I would do the same thing every day when I dropped her off, even down to using the same language. So I would chat to her on the way in and then say, 'I need to go now so see you later' and then a member of staff would be available to take my daughter from me – she rarely went willingly which made the goodbyes difficult. Then I would leave the building and turn back to see my daughter who would be looking out of the window with the adult waiting for me to walk past. I would smile, wave and blow kisses and then walk home. I usually managed to hold it together until I was out of sight, but then my own tears flowed! This was a very difficult phase, which continued for a few years, but thankfully she grew out of it by the time she entered junior school.

Insecure attachments

Ainsworth and colleagues grouped how children responded to their caregivers and their research led to identifying different types of attachments. They found that in addition to children with secure attachments who display a typical pattern of attachment behaviour, there are also children who have an insecure attachment. Children respond in slightly different ways depending on which attachment style they have. For example, children with an anxious-avoidant attachment may not have separation anxiety but would not show any interest in their parent when they return, whereas children with an anxious-resistant attachment would have a severe response to their parent leaving but may reject their parent when they return (Ainsworth et al., 1978). A group of children with a disorganised attachment might be totally unpredictable in their attachment behaviour which is confusing and erratic. This attachment style is the most challenging form of insecure attachment and is often associated with abuse, neglect or inconsistent parenting styles (Main & Solomon, 1986).

It is worth noting that the same child can react differently and display various attachment behaviours at times depending on their circumstances. For example, if their main carer became ill or the family circumstances changed. In addition, there are many contributions to insecure attachments: some may be issues during early childhood or even issues during pregnancy. Sometimes we may never know why some children have insecure attachments. Despite this, having an understanding of attachment theory and how we can build secure attachments is an important part of our role. This is because how securely attached a child feels also has a direct influence on their behaviour.

Building secure attachments

As explained above, if children have a strong bond with an adult who cares for them, they will feel confident to participate in setting life. However, some children will find it more difficult to build these relationships and we need to be aware of this, adapt our expectations accordingly and strive to build secure attachments with our children.

Strategies to support children to build secure attachments:

- Spend time together, use positive touch and make eye contact with our children.
- Closely observe children, tune into them and listen to them, responding to their needs and wants sensitively.
- Remain calm and use a warm and friendly tone of voice.

- Smile regularly and remain animated when talking with them.
- Find out their interests and fascinations and tap into these to personalise provision.
- Have a consistent routine which offers structure and predictability.
- Use visual timetables, objects of reference and signs to support communication.
- Have realistic expectations of behaviour and ensure a consistent approach (home and setting) with regular reassurance from adults.
- Allow specific toys or comforters to help children feel secure.
- Create a sense of belonging through displays and photos.
- Offer safe spaces and areas of retreat for children.
- Have a setting pet which the children can help to look after.

FEELING SAFE AND SECURE – A PRESCHOOL'S PERSPECTIVE

After the first lockdown, we were reflecting on the effectiveness of the setting's provision in relation to children's wellbeing. We wanted to support our children to feel more safe and secure and we decided to invest in pets for the children to look after. We researched ideas and theory on animal therapy and found that early experiences of pets and animal care promotes children's wellbeing and stimulates empathy and caring. In some cases animals can be used to settle children's emotions, provide positive reinforcements for behaviour and help them to develop self-regulation.

We chose to buy two guinea pigs which the children were really excited to play with. We even ran a fundraiser to name them! We are based on a school site and soon after we got the guinea pigs we received this letter from the school mentor:

After an emotionally draining day, I went to see the guinea pigs to decompress and take my mind off what had happened that afternoon. I find animals really calming and cuddling them really made me smile and feel better. Their vulnerability also made me feel needed! It was a definite distraction watching them running

around and exploring their new home. Being there helped clear my mind and enabled me to reset.

I think having the guinea pigs will be beneficial for the children for several reasons:

- having something to take care of and look after teaches children responsibility
- being able to talk to an animal without a response helps children communicate without fear of rejection or ridicule
- behaving appropriately around the guinea pigs will help instil good manners and behaviour in the children
- cuddling and stroking an animal can release endorphins making the children feel happier or more relaxed
- watching and playing with the guinea pigs will be fun and some children may not have this opportunity at home
- focusing on something else exciting and different could help the children move past any negative emotions they might be feeling.

Since their arrival, children and adults from across the preschool and school have visited the guinea pigs to support their emotional wellbeing and the animals have given the whole school community a positive mood uplift, offering a little excitement during a difficult phase.

Feeling safe and secure

Most people have come across Maslow's hierarchy of needs (1943) and the human need for safety is the second on his list. Once people have satisfied their physiological needs like hunger and thirst, they will want to feel safe and secure. He talks about the desire for predictability, stability and routine. 'We may generalize and say that the average child in our society generally prefers a safe, orderly, predictable, organized world, which he can count on, and in which unexpected, unmanageable or other dangerous things do not happen...' (Maslow, 1943, p. 378). He goes on to talk about the role of parents in shielding and protecting our children in this. He also says that the average healthy adult does not have any safety needs because generally speaking they are safe in their day-to-day life. However, Maslow also acknowledges that if a child has been subjected to traumatic events, such as abuse, divorce or death of a family member they may feel less safe and their previous stable world may become unstable.

Adverse childhood experiences

This links with what we now call ACEs which stands for adverse childhood experiences. These are traumatic events that a child might experience which have a negative impact on their lives, for example domestic violence, being the victim of abuse or neglect, parental separation or divorce, a family member being in prison, or affected by drug or alcohol misuse. There has now been a wealth of research which confirms that if a child has experienced several ACEs this will have a negative impact on their lives into adulthood. It can even affect their physical health, wellbeing and the likelihood of their being violent themselves or engaging in criminal or harmful acts (Collingwood et al., 2018).

ACEs can cause 'toxic stress' which is when our bodies experience stress for prolonged periods and we are unable to control the stress levels. At this point we have a high level of the stress hormone cortisol in our bodies and too much of this hormone is harmful to us. A small amount of cortisol is a natural response and can even be helpful; however, if we continually experience too much stress, this has a very negative impact on our developing brains and mental and physical health and wellbeing.

ACEs are really common, with one UK study finding that over 47% of people have experienced one or more ACE in childhood and over 12% have experienced four or more (Bellis et al., 2013). This research concluded that ACEs contribute to poorer health and social outcomes and people who have experienced four or more ACEs are at greater risk of violence, early unplanned pregnancy, incarceration and unemployment. They also found that these risks were passed on to the next generation as their own children were more likely to be exposed to ACEs.

There is a little good news, as Collingwood et al. note: 'Early action and prevention can have a profoundly positive impact upon health, educational and criminal outcomes, improving the long-term outcomes for individuals and families, but also increasing the nation's cultural, societal and financial capital' (2018, p.5). So there are many preventative measures that can be put in place which can help limit the impact of ACEs or even prevent some ACEs. Early childhood educators play a key role in this by providing a predictable and stable environment, building secure and nurturing attachments and helping children to develop skills, like resilience, which will help them to overcome the various challenges that life deals them.

Trauma and attachment aware practice

It is vital that our settings are trauma and attachment aware with informed educators who understand how ACEs and attachment impact children's lives and know how to prevent or minimise the impact of them. Collingwood et al. (2018) use the example of a bank when thinking about how the main caregiver can raise or lower a child's wellbeing. Most of the time the adult is paying into the account and the child's wellbeing is increased; however, there will be times when they make a withdrawal. This could be because the parent is unwell or stressed. If the child's balance is high, they will be able to withstand this without too much impact; however, if the child began their life with a very low balance or were even overdrawn to begin with, due to adverse conditions during pregnancy, it is clear to see how this would have a knock-on effect for the child. Some children have such a deficit that they may never get a good credit rating in terms of wellbeing. Our role as early childhood educators is to pay into children's wellbeing accounts as much as we can.

One great way to do this is to adopt an ethos in our settings of bucket filling! There are a series of books aimed at young children which explain how our actions and words impact other people. They share the story that each of us carry an invisible bucket and we can either fill or empty our own and other people's buckets by our actions and words. Kind actions and words fill buckets, unkind actions and words empty buckets.

BEING A BUCKET FILLER

A reception teacher's perspective

We used the book *Have You Filled a Bucket Today?* by Carol McCloud (2015) after a parent recommended it. In the current climate and with the transition of children returning to school after lockdown it sounded perfect. I bought it and took it into school the very next day to read it as our daily 'Tell a Tale'. The children's response to the book was amazing; you could have heard a pin drop and they were intrigued as to how they could fill their own bucket and each other's bucket. What was even more surprising was that not one child mentioned how their bucket could be emptied so I took this as a real positive. We talked for the rest of the day about how a good deed that they had carried out had just filled their bucket and another child's bucket. The children were desperate to talk about the kind things they had done at school and at home and the following day I asked them if they had filled any buckets at home. The book has so much potential and could be used as a display throughout the year that we could add to. We hope to buy buckets that the children could write their kind deed on paper and place in the bucket (mark making to begin with). We could then share these at the end of each day. The book is still referred to now, a few months on, and it is such a positive, child-friendly way of reinforcing kindness in the classroom, in the playground, around school and at home.

A nursery teacher's perspective

We read *Fill a Bucket* (Martin, 2017) which comes before *Have You Filled a Bucket Today?* (McCloud, 2015). My nursery children love it every year. They soon learn that we use our feelings to 'fill our own and other people's buckets'. They often say, 'Did that fill your bucket?' We use it to support our PSHE curriculum and raise self-esteem, support friendships, feelings, and promote team work.

A preschool teacher's perspective

My children are aged 3–4 years and after sharing the story about bucket filling, we had a sand bucket pinned to the wall with heart-shaped sticky paper and a pen accessible to the children. Adults modelled writing things such as 'I would like to thank (name) for tidying up after snack and filling my bucket'. Children would then ask an adult to scribe their messages or draw something to add to the bucket. This was a way of celebrating and sharing the kind and caring behaviour we saw at preschool.

A childminder's perspective

I was recommended this book as a way of discussing challenging behaviour with children when I had a specific child in mind. I read it to a group of 3–4 year olds and the child in question latched onto the concept so well that I gave them the copy to keep and ordered several more! After reading it we discussed the concept and got some buckets to fill with things that made us smile. The children occasionally link another's behaviour to the story during their play, for example, 'Don't break my tower or you'll empty my bucket!'

There are many ways that we can be trauma and attachment aware in our practice, for example:

- Ensure all educators in our team understand about attachment, trauma and ACEs and include reference to this approach in our setting's policies.
- Prioritise wellbeing for staff and children.
- Ensure that our key person approach is effective and have a buddy key person system in place if needed.
- Build secure attachments with children and get to know their families and their backgrounds.
- Be reliable, trustworthy and dependable and role model a calm attitude.
- Have an open-door policy for parents and carers and always be there for children.

- Provide a loving, safe and secure environment and relaxed and welcoming ethos where every child and family matters.
- Offer predictable routines and consistent behavioural expectations.
- Provide opportunities during the day when we can check in with children.
- Work closely with parents and carers, find out about any changes at home and encourage consistency between home and setting.
- See transitions as part of the day and plan for them, especially arrivals and departures.
- Allow the use of transitional objects or comforters if needed.
- Plan for our emotional environment in terms of activities, stories and displays.
- Use emotion coaching approaches to support children and teach skills such as problem solving.
- Offer lots of opportunities for children to become more independent learners.
- Accept that separation anxiety is a 'normal' part of secure attachments and will not last forever and remember that parental separation anxiety can also arise.
- Reframe 'attention-seeking' children as 'attachment-seeking' children.
- Provide calming areas and use sensory resources and calming strategies, finding out which work well for specific children.
- Provide visual timetables, Now/Next boards and visual cues to help children understand the routine of the day.
- Avoid public praise or reward systems built on social compliance. Instead use labelled praise and encouragement.

 **ACTIVITY**

Reflecting upon the various factors that could potentially prevent children from feeling safe and secure can be a useful activity to help us be proactive in supporting them, particularly if we consider how we can respond and what we can do about it. Below is an example of a table which includes some of these factors. Have a go at completing more rows adding our own factors and writing down clear actions of how we can respond.

Factors that prevent children from feeling safe and secure	Response: What we can do about these factors
Coronavirus	
ACEs	
New baby	
Moving home	

Concluding thoughts

In this chapter we have thought about the importance of enabling children to feel safe and secure and the impact that this will have on their social, emotional and mental health (SEMH). Children need to feel this way before they are ready to learn. We also know that there are many factors that can get in the way of this sense of security, for example experiencing ACEs. Having a secure knowledge and understanding of how trauma, attachment and ACEs can impact our children will enable us to better support them. The next chapter explores additional reasons why children may behave the way they do.

QUESTIONS FOR REFLECTION

In what ways do we use our knowledge of attachment theory and trauma to support the children in our care?

How can we 'invest' in our children and make deposits in their emotional bank accounts?

How can we help children feel more safe and secure in our setting?

Further reading

Brooks, R. (2020) *The Trauma and Attachment Aware Classroom*. London: Jessica Kingsley Publishers.

Collingwood, S., Knox, A., Fowler, H., Harding, S., Irwin, S. & Quinney, S. (2018) *The Little Book of Adverse Childhood Experiences*. Imagination Lancaster. Retrieved from www.saferbradford.co.uk/media/4sff2jsx/little-book-of-aces.pdf

Read, V. (2014) *Developing Attachment in Early Years Settings: Nurturing Secure Relationships from Birth to Five Years*, 2nd edn. Abingdon: Routledge.

References

Ainsworth, M., Blehar, M., Waters, E. & Wall, S. (1978) *Patterns of Attachment: A Psychological Study of the Strange Situation.* Mahwah, NJ: Lawrence Erlbaum.

Bellis, M., Lowey, H., Leckenby, N., Hughes, K. & Harrison, D. (2013) Adverse childhood experiences: Retrospective study to determine their impact on adult health behaviours and health outcomes in a UK population. *Journal of Public Health,* 36(1), 81–91.

Bergin, C. & Bergin, D. (2009) Attachment in the classroom. *Educational Psychology Review,* 21, 141–170.

Bowlby, J. (1988) *A Secure Base: Clinical Applications of Attachment Theory.* London: Taylor & Francis.

Collingwood, S., Knox, A., Fowler, H., Harding, S., Irwin, S. & Quinney, S. (2018) *The Little Book of Adverse Childhood Experiences.* Imagination Lancaster. Retrieved from www.saferbradford.co.uk/media/4sff2jsx/little-book-of-aces.pdf

Holmes, J. (2014) *John Bowlby and Attachment Theory.* London: Routledge.

Karst, P. (2018) *The Invisible String.* New York: Little, Brown Young Readers.

Main, M. & Solomon, J. (1986) Discovery of a new, insecure-disorganized/disoriented attachment pattern. In T. B. Brazelton & M. Yogman (eds), *Affective Development in Infancy.* New York: Ablex.

Martin, K. (2017) *Fill a Bucket: A Guide to Daily Happiness for Young Children.* Chicago, IL: Bucket Fillosophy.

Maslow, A. H. (1943) A theory of human motivation. *Psychological Review,* 50(4), 370–396.

McCloud, C. (2015) *Have You Filled a Bucket Today? A Guide to Daily Happiness for Kids.* Chicago, IL: Bucket Fillers.

Waddell, M. (1992) *Owl Babies.* London: Walker Books.

Why children behave the way they do

This chapter will present a number of different reasons why children behave the way they do. It will share the characteristics of children during conflict situations or when they behave in challenging ways. It will explain about the natural emotional response that happens in our brains and how we are unable to think when our emotions overtake us.

Introduction

In order to respond appropriately to children's behaviour we need to do everything we can to understand the child and the context they find themselves in and unpick why they behave the way they do. Thinking about the why helps us to assess the situation and will also help us to use appropriate strategies when we respond. Observation is key to this understanding and getting to know our children really well is a good place to start.

Considering why children behave the way they do gives us an insight into their world. Unless the child tells us why, we can never be 100 per cent certain when working this out, so we must always remain tentative in our assertions, thinking, 'Perhaps it is because of this…' or 'Maybe it is because of that…' This will help us not to make assumptions about their behaviour and jump to the wrong conclusions. Sometimes we will never know the reason for the behaviour, and that's OK. This chapter aims to explore the characteristics of young children when they behave in challenging ways and also think about why they might behave that way in the first place. Chapter 5 builds on these ideas and invites us to become behaviour detectives to work out why

DOI: 10.4324/9781003137474-3

children behave the way they do, and Chapter 6 considers a range of strategies that educators can adopt to support their children.

Dysregulation

During our day there might be several times when children get upset, cross, throw a toy inappropriately or shout in anger. Sometimes a child will have a bad day with us and we have a quick catch up with the parent at the end of the day and they say, 'Oh, sorry, he had a really late night last night…' and we think to ourselves that this explains everything! On reflection, after the event, it can be easier to work out why things escalated. I am referring to this as times of stress rather than poor behaviour because this reminds us how these situations may make a child feel stressed and dysregulated.

We all have times and days when we are emotionally dysregulated and out of sorts. Dysregulation is a term used to describe a person who is 'not themselves' or anxious or full of emotion. It describes the freeze, fight or flight mode that I will explain more fully below. Usually when someone is dysregulated, they are unable to think rationally, they may have a low sense of wellbeing and are not OK. If a child is dysregulated, they will not be ready to learn.

What is going on in our brains?

When we are calm, emotionally regulated and generally feeling OK, our upstairs brain, as Siegel and Bryson call it, is in control (2012). We can think before we act, empathise and make decisions. However, during times of stress, when we are dysregulated, the downstairs brain takes over and the thinking part of our brain is not fully in control. At this point we have overpowering emotions and go into 'freeze, flight or fight' mode. This is a survival technique. Years ago, we might have needed to hide from a predator, run away from danger or fight for food. Our bodies rush with adrenaline and our brain fills with cortisol, the stress hormone. This is not a good place to be!

Before we can carry on with our day, we need to calm down and regulate our emotions again. Everyone's brains react in this way and, as adults, we have had lots of practice in learning how to respond. For example, we might take a deep breath or ring our bestie to let off steam. Sadly, most young children have not yet learned how to deal with these feelings, so young children can appear emotionally dysregulated more than others. We need to acknowledge that this natural response happens and plan for it whilst also using calming techniques with children before we can begin to resolve any issues.

Causes of stress

There are many reasons why we get over emotional and dysregulated in the first place. Several of these are due to child development and children not yet being fully able to cope with the emotional, social and cognitive demands of a typical day. Other reasons may be due to past experiences or changes in the home or setting. I have listed several causes of stress in our settings and shared a brief example from the adult or child's perspective below. These causes and stressors are unpicked in more detail in the following section:

- Unmet basic needs – 'I'm hungry…' 'I'm tired…'
- Adverse childhood experiences (ACEs) and trauma – 'He witnessed domestic violence…'
- Lack of communication – 'You don't understand…'
- Frustration – 'I want to do it myself…'
- Not yet learned the boundaries or rules – 'She said, "No!" yesterday, I wonder what she'll say today…'
- Lack of Theory of Mind and empathy – 'How will Sarah feel if you take her toy?'
- Attention seeking – 'I want you to play with me…'
- Space – 'I haven't got a space on the carpet…'
- Fairness – 'It's not fair!'
- Privilege – 'He always gets to play on the iPad…'
- Social – 'You're not coming to my birthday party…'
- Resourcing or fighting over a toy – 'I had it first…' 'It's mine!'
- Adult timescale – 'It's snack time now…'
- Finding waiting difficult – 'Is it my turn yet?'

- Transitions – 'Time to tidy up…'
- Changes in the setting – 'Your key person isn't here today…'
- Changes at home – 'I have a new baby at home…'
- Bereavement – 'Sadly, his Grandma passed away at the weekend…'
- Upset prior to attending that day – 'We ran out of Shreddies…'
- Schematic play – 'He throws everything!'
- Boredom – 'She's running around like crazy and won't settle to anything…'
- Weather – 'It's so windy out there!'

You can probably think of even more reasons to add to this list. We could look at several stressors on this list and feel unable to do anything about them; some are developmental or home/environmental issues and some are just situations that arise and are difficult to prevent. Although we may not be able to directly prevent or control these situations, we must continually respond with empathy, understanding and support.

Children will respond to these stressors in a number of different ways, many of which will challenge us, and it can be difficult to know the best way to react. This next section will look at each of these stressors and offer a few pointers on how to respond positively. Chapter 6 explores lots of the strategies mentioned below in more detail.

Unmet basic needs

I can't count the number of times that I have said to a parent at the end of the day, 'XXX has been very grumpy today' only to find that they had a late night or had woken in the night with a bad dream. Chapter 1 explores the importance of feeling safe and secure but I wish I'd learned earlier in my career how vital it was to meet children's basic needs. Although I had studied Maslow (1943) and his hierarchy of needs during my training, I hadn't grasped just how something like being hungry or tired could really impact behaviour. I have since learned that it is vital to have a good relationship with parents and carers and to establish a morning routine which includes checking in with families as they arrive. We need to know if they've had a late night or skipped breakfast and then we can do something about it. We can amend our routine to allow more rest time, offer the child breakfast or even bring their snack forward. These little things will make a huge differ-ence for individual children.

Adverse childhood experiences and trauma

As Chapter 1 has explored, sadly some children will arrive in our settings having had ACEs or trauma. ACEs include a number of different traumatic and difficult experiences such as abuse, parental separation or living with a drug user or alcoholic. Research has shown that ACEs can lead to toxic stress which is when our stress levels are dangerously high and will impact on our physical health and mental wellbeing. We must ensure we remain trauma and attachment aware in our practice to support our children.

Lack of communication

Communication and language develop rapidly in a child's first three years and children's understanding of language develops in advance of their speech, so children will understand much more than they can say. Many of the children we are working with will have little or no spoken language and it can be difficult for them to express themselves or feel understood. This can lead to feelings of frustration, which, in turn, can lead to children behav-ing inappropriately. If we view this behaviour as communication, what they are really saying is, 'I don't understand' or 'You don't understand me'. We need to respond sensitively and with empathy, do all we can to relieve this frustration and develop children's language and communication skills, and the poor behaviour will diminish.

Frustration

Children may also feel very frustrated when their physical skills do not quite match what they want to do. The prime time for children's gross motor skills to develop is from antenatal to about 5 years old, whilst the prime time for their fine motor skills is from shortly after birth to about age 9. So many children will want to do something that they will find physically challenging and the result is a frustrated child who plays up. Again, our response needs to be very sensitive and if we can break down the task into smaller steps it might help.

HELPING A CHILD TO ACHIEVE – A CHILDMINDER'S PERSPECTIVE

We looked after a 2 year old who always wanted to do everything themselves. Any time you tried to help she shouted, 'Me do it!' and would even run away from the adult at times. We found she would get very frustrated and that's when we would struggle with her behaviour. We realised that she wasn't meaning to be difficult, she was just frustrated that she couldn't do what she wanted to. When we observed her more, we realised one of the areas where she struggled was putting her coat on and we noticed that her hand–eye coordination and fine motor control wasn't quite up to the task so we tried to offer her some strategies to help. We demonstrated the upside down technique for putting coats on, and held the zip still when she tried to put the other half of the zip in. During our session we introduced lots of fine motor play, such as playdough, large tweezers in the messy play area, different fasteners on role play clothing and a locks board, where children were invited to unlock several padlocks and bolts to 'rescue' a toy. Over time and with understanding from us, she became more confident at managing tasks herself and cries of, 'Me do it!' became a thing of the past!

Not yet learned the boundaries or rules

It takes a long time to understand rules and when children are developing a sense of self they will want to push the boundaries at times. This is to be expected and planned for. We can support our children by having a consistent routine and offer gentle reminders. We also need to have realistic expectations – our children will not always understand or respect the boundaries and rules. Chapter 3 looks at this in more detail.

Lack of Theory of Mind and empathy

Theory of Mind is our ability to predict mental states and when we understand that other people have thoughts and feelings that are different to our own. We could say that empathy is Theory of Mind in action. Sometimes our expectations for children may not be developmentally appropriate. We cannot expect all our children to be able to empathise, or know how certain actions would impact others before they happen. These things are out of reach for a child who is still developing Theory of Mind, and Chapter 3 explores and explains this.

Attention/attachment seeking

Sometimes children behave in a certain way to gain our attention. If we think about what they are aiming to achieve by behaving in this way, it is to be noticed by us, to love and connect with us! I find it helpful to imagine that everyone has a sort of emotional cup – when it is full, we feel happy, loved and can cope with the demands of the world; however, when it is empty, we feel emotionally exhausted, in need of attention and unsure if we are loved (Chapman & Campbell, 2012). Children who use attention-seeking behaviour have an empty cup and need more attention. So it is helpful to think of this, rather than as *attention* seeking, as *attachment* seeking, and in giving them attention we are filling their emotional cup. This immediately helps us to feel more positive about this type of behaviour.

Space

I've always found that children need lots of space! Yet in our settings we tend to cram children together and expect them to sit and not fiddle with each other, for example during storytime on the carpet or in an assembly. This will inevitably lead to problems so it should come as no surprise that children will struggle if they do not feel they have enough space. We can plan for this issue by having developmentally appropriate expectations of our children and accepting if they are sitting too close together some children may struggle. Chapter 3 looks at our expectations in more detail.

Fairness

Children have a real sense of justice, injustice, fairness and rules, regardless of whether or not they keep the rules themselves! Things can appear unfair to children because they do not see the bigger picture. For example, we might know that we do not have time for all children to share during a session, so we ask two children to share. However, without an understanding of time, this may look unfair or like preferential treatment for someone else. From the child's perspective they might feel that we like the other child more than them. Whenever possible we need to explain our reasons for responding or acting the way we do so that we are helping children to understand a little more about the bigger picture.

Privilege

This is linked to fairness. Children do not want to feel they are getting a raw deal and they will notice small things, like who was the first in line last time or who always gets to have a turn on novel things like iPads. From our adult perspective, we might want a particular child to lead the line because they are sensible or we might allow another child some time on an iPad to occupy them during a tricky moment. We do not always fully explain these reasons to our children, however we need to be careful that the message we're giving to our children isn't saying I favour them over you.

Social

From the moment we are born we seek out interaction and are constantly learning how to connect with others. Despite being social from birth, children find collaboration difficult. In fact, developmentally children under about 2 ½ will not play cooperatively with each other. Children older than this are learning how to play with others and will need adult support to help them. Occasionally we hear children socially exclude others from their play, for example we may hear them say, 'You're not coming to my birthday party' or 'Girls can't climb trees…' We must be aware when children have social disagreements and ensure that we challenge any stereotypes or discrimination if we come across it. Chapter 3 looks at developmentally appropriate expectations with regard to social development.

Resourcing or fighting over a toy

We've all heard the cry, 'I had it first…' or 'It's mine!' and had to step in when a tug of war ensues. This is a really common issue in our settings and it arises because, as mentioned above, very young children find cooperative play difficult. Sharing is an abstract concept and very difficult for young children to understand, let alone do. As adults we rarely share anything, yet we expect sometimes very young children to share toys and resources and get upset when they don't! Finding sharing and playing cooperatively with others difficult is a normal part of growing up and therefore, as educators, we need to allow children time and opportunities to resolve such issues themselves. Chapter 3 goes into a little more detail about how we can support children to share in developmentally appropriate ways.

Adult timescale

Sometimes incidents arise in our setting due to an adult-imposed timescale. For example, when I was childminding, if I was collecting children from preschool at a certain time, the younger children had to interrupt their play which sometimes led to an upset. Strategies that I used to help with this were using a visual timetable, offering a prompt reminding them that we need to collect soon and using sand timers to help show the passage of time. Again, this is not poor behaviour, this is adults getting in the way of the serious nature of play!

Finding waiting difficult

In addition, some difficult behaviours occur if our routine has too much sedentary time or necessitates the children to wait at different points in the day, for example if all children need to wash their hands at the same time. Young children find it difficult to wait, even if they are waiting for something lovely; this is linked with self-regulation and is explored further in Chapter 7. Strategies to support this include limiting sedentary or waiting time as much as possible, making waiting fun and engaging through singing a song, doing an action rhyme or altering our routine slightly to avoid bottlenecks – for example by grouping children to wash hands rather than sending them all at once.

Transitions

Young children find change very difficult, which is why routine is so important. Times of transition can be stressful for both adults and children and we sometimes find they are trigger points for poor behaviour. In order to avoid this, we need to plan for transitions and see them as part of the day, rather than linking times. So plan for and allow extra time for transitions, offering prompts prior to any changes occurring, e.g. 'Five more minutes then we tidy up'. Time is an abstract concept so using sand or liquid timers can also help children to see time passing in a more visual way.

Changes in the setting or at home

As mentioned above, change is difficult for young children to cope with. Sometimes there will be unavoidable changes in our settings, for example if their key person is ill and not at work. In addition to this, changes happening at home will also have a big impact on the child. It could be something lovely like a new baby or unsettling like a house move. There are too many potential changes both in the setting and at home to list here; however, when change happens we need to respond sensitively and try to keep our routines as consistent as possible to offer the child more security. We should talk about any changes with our children, regardless of their age, but do so in a developmentally appropriate way. We can also work closely with parents and carers and try to establish some consistency between home and setting. Chapter 9 considers how we can develop effective partnerships with others.

Bereavement

Sadly, death is a part of life, so at some point our children will experience loss. We need to help prepare them for this rather than shelter them from it, so we should talk with our children about death and what this means, being as honest as possible, using terms that are factual and portray information, which avoids the potential for misunderstandings. If you are caring for a child who is not your own, you must liaise with their family and ensure that you discuss how you will approach this topic sensitively. There are lots of excellent resources on the market to help us support children and families who are bereaved with expert help available should we need it. A few books that come highly recommended are *Always and Forever* by Alan Durant (2013), *Badger's Parting Gifts* by Susan Varley (1987) and *Waterbugs and Dragonflies* by Doris Stickney (2019).

Upset prior to attending that day

Sometimes the small things can be quite traumatic or upsetting for our youngest children. Simply running out of their favourite cereal in the morning could make them out of sorts for the day. I expect you can think of a time when you have noticed a child is not themselves all day and when you speak to parents about this, you find out that they had a row with their elder brother that morning or the dog is really ill and has gone to the vets... It is really helpful to have a good relationship with parents and carers so that we find out about any upsets that may have happened before they arrive in our setting for the session.

Schematic play

I am always saddened by how often schematic play is misdiagnosed as misbehaviour. A child will be engaging in repetitive play, for example throwing everything they engage with, and this is immediately seen as poor behaviour. Instead, we need to observe the child closely and ask the question – could this be schematic? That helps us to reframe what they are doing and see it in a more positive light. Chapter 8 looks into this in more detail.

Boredom

Another reason why children may behave inappropriately is because they are bored and not inspired by anything we are providing for them. Using the Leuven Scale for Wellbeing and Involvement can help us to measure how engaged children are in our setting at different times of the day (Laevers, 2005). Then we can review our continuous provision and think about how we can introduce challenge or tap into children's interests more effectively to increase their motivation levels. Setting up some provocations, or *invitations to learn* as I call them, can help. If we make our learning environment inviting and stimulating there will be less time for poor behaviour. When considering children's motivation, Griffard suggests that we need to consider the thrill factor which will engage children and then we can develop children's skills (2010).

ENGAGING OUR CHILDREN – A PRESCHOOL'S PERSPECTIVE

One year we had a cohort of really boisterous children. At any given opportunity they would run about or ride the scooters and crash into the wall. This became difficult to manage and we were concerned that an accident was waiting to happen. We realised that our children were bored. We were not providing anything engaging enough for them to want to sustain attention. So we reviewed our continuous provision and created a woodwork area and an obstacle course for the ride-ons to navigate and generally made our provision more challenging for this group. We found that levels of engagement rose and we were no longer seeing mindless running or crashing games.

Weather

Believe it or not but the weather appears to affect children's behaviour! On a really windy day children are more excited than on a calm, sunny day! One research study found that we can predict the mood of people by looking at the weather. On days with more hours of sunshine people tend to be more optimistic and on very humid days people tend to feel more sleepy. Anecdotally I have noticed that my mood and the children's mood are affected by the weather. On a stormy day with high winds the children will be more hyper in the setting and on a bright, sunny day they will appear happier. A thunderstorm can send some children over the edge, some will feel very excited, whilst others will be very frightened. We need to respond sensitively.

 **ACTIVITY**

Write down the names of your key children and note next to them if you have any ideas of why they behave the way they do or if any of these things influence their behaviour. If you are not sure, do a focused observation with the ideas from this chapter in mind.

Concluding thoughts

As this chapter has shown, there is always a reason and a variety of different stressors and causes for the way children behave. Our role as educators is to try to understand, empathise and respond appropriately to our children. Usually challenging behaviour is accompanied by big feelings, and therefore children will need their feelings validated. In order to fully support our children we need to get to know them well, work out what motivates and fascinates them as well as what upsets and frustrates them. Then we can use this information to plan engaging, exciting and developmentally appropriate activities and there will be less time for challenging behaviour. The next chapter explores this idea as we consider having realistic expectations of our children.

QUESTIONS FOR REFLECTION

Is our practice influenced by our understanding of what happens in our brains?

Have we thought about the reasons why children behave the way they do?

What do we need to change in the light of this chapter?

Further reading

I have written several articles and blogs about why children behave the way they do. They can be found on my website at www.tam-singrimmer.com/behaviour-emotion

Mathieson, K. (2015) *Understanding Behaviour in the Early Years*. London: MA Education.

Tassoni, P. (2018) *Understanding Children's Behaviour: Learning to Be with Others in the Early Years*. London: Featherstone.

References

Chapman, G. & Campbell, R. (2012) *The 5 love languages of children*. Chicago, IL: Northfield Publishing.

Durant, A. (2013) *Always and Forever*. London: Picture Corgi.

Griffard, P. B. (2010) Dissecting motivation: The will-skill-thrill profile. *Journal of College Science Teaching*, 40(1), 10–11.

Laevers, F. (2005) *Well-Being and Involvement in Care Settings: A Process-Oriented Self-Evaluation Instrument.* Leuven: Kind & Gezin and Research Centre for Experiential Education.

Maslow, A. H. (1943) A theory of human motivation. *Psychological Review*, 50(4), 370–396.

Seigel, D. & Bryson, T. (2012) *The Whole Brain Child.* London: Robinson.

Stickney, D. (2019) *Water Bugs and Dragonflies: Explaining Death to Young Children.* London: Bloomsbury Continuum.

Varley, S. (1987) *Badger's Parting Gifts.* London: Anderson Press.

Realistic expectations

This chapter will explore the expectations we have for our children and why it is vital they are realistic and developmentally appropriate. Unpicking concepts like sharing in a developmentally appropriate way, it will share age-stage expectations relating to behaviour in line with typical development, whilst explaining that emotionally many children will not work at this typical level.

Introduction

Imagine that your headteacher or senior manager calls you into the office and says, 'We've just had the call from the inspectors! They are arriving tomorrow and before they get here I want you to change all the displays in your room, re-label all the resources, organise the storage shed outside, write thorough plans for your teaching over the next couple of days, make sure that your floor books are up to date. It's too short notice to cancel parent's evening that is planned from 5–9pm tonight I'm afraid. You'll get it all done, I have every faith in you!' Talk about unrealistic expectations! We could do a few of these things on a normal evening, but to fit them in around parent's evening would be impossible! We are likely to feel stressed, upset or even angry that we are expected to do these unattainable things.

Sometimes we have unrealistic expectations of our children. We expect them to be able to sit and wait their turn, share with others or understand how other people might feel, when these things are often developmentally out of their reach. We expect too much of them and set them and us up for a fall. This chapter will consider some of the

DOI: 10.4324/9781003137474-4

behavioural expectations we place on our children and think about them in terms of child development.

Understanding child development

In order to have developmentally appropriate expectations we must ensure that we know and understand how children learn and develop from birth to 5, and think about them in terms of not only their age but also their stage of development. This is where professional development comes in. Managers and senior leaders must ensure their staff have access to high-quality training and professional development opportunities and training should always be disseminated across the whole setting.

Within the Early Years Foundation Stage we have an excellent resource which can help us to think about children's age and stage of development called *Birth to Five Matters*. This is a non-statutory guidance document written by the sector which helps us to implement the EYFS in our settings. The first section shares quality and effective practice, but the bulk of the document is dedicated to trajectories or tables relating to areas of learning and development and is divided into developmental stages. For each area we can look at the unique child section, what children might be doing, and then consider how we could support them in terms of enabling environments and positive relationships. (The document and additional information can be accessed for free at www.birthto5matters.org.uk.) There are also some really helpful books which look at child development at different ages and stages as well as websites.

Developmentally appropriate expectations

It is important that we consider our children in relation to typical development, so thinking about the children we look after and feeling confident that our expectations are developmentally appropriate is vital. It might help to bear developmental milestones in mind. A developmental milestone is an ability that is achieved by most children by a certain age. They can involve physical, social, emotional, behavioural, cognitive and communication skills such as walking, sharing with others, expressing emotions, self-soothing, recognising familiar sounds and talking.

The following table includes examples from practice of typical milestones. It does not cover everything but, hopefully, gives us an idea of what each area could include. It is important to understand that these areas overlap and it is difficult to compartmentalise learning and development. Theory of Mind, discussed below, would fit into both the social and cognitive areas and self-regulation would be in both emotional and behavioural. It doesn't really matter how we categorise these milestones, but what does matter is understanding and applying developmentally appropriate practice.

Developmental area	Example of typical milestone
Physical	Holding head up, rolling over, crawling, walking
Cognitive	Responding to facial expressions, recognising their name, learning number names, Theory of Mind
Social	Smiling, imitating others, playing collaboratively, Theory of Mind
Emotional	Expressing emotions and feelings, self-regulation
Behavioural	Self-soothing, self-regulation
Communication	Non-verbal communication, language acquisition

We need to know about typical development for many reasons, but primarily so that we can intervene early if we have any concerns about a child. However, it is important to remember that all children develop at different rates and no two children will be identical. Tables and trajectories give us an idea of the age range when most children will do or achieve certain things, but they must not be taken as 100% accurate for every child. Child development is not linear and does not progress incrementally; sometimes children may even regress or appear to make accelerated progress and this is OK. It is also important to discuss child development with parents and carers and find out as much as we can about their previous development prior to being in our setting. This can sometimes build up a picture of a child's development and prove invaluable. If we have any concerns at all about a child's development we must share this with others, whether our SENCo in our setting or with a health visitor.

As early childhood educators we want to plan effective learning environments that tap into children's interests and enable them to learn effectively. Understanding about developmentally appropriate practice can help us to do this. It is not just about ensuring we have resources or an enabling environment aimed at a particular age and stage of development, but also about having expectations about children's behaviour that fit within these ages and stages. I think this creates a more respectful environment that empowers children and links with some of the ideas I shared in my book *Developing a Loving Pedagogy in the Early Years* when I talk about empowering children through love: the balance of power between adults and children, actively listening to children, offering them advocacy and agency, contributing to their sense of self-efficacy, offering unconditional love and being led by the child (Grimmer, 2021).

REALISTIC EXPECTATIONS – A NURSERY'S PERSPECTIVE

Our nursery always used to pride itself on having high expectations for all children, until we met 4 year old William! His teachers were finding it difficult to cope with his behaviour because he seemed incapable of sitting still, lining up and waiting his turn. During morning carpet time, William would begin sitting with the other children, but within a few minutes he was fiddling with his shoes or the toys in the cupboard behind him or rolling around on the floor. We tried several strategies from moving him to giving him his own carpet square to sit on. Although this helped a little, William usually ended up being removed from the session due to his disruptive behaviour. We also noticed that William would not want to line up with the other children to wash his hands before lunch and during session time he would want to play outside all day and never come inside and sit at the table to do any learning. William even used to find waiting difficult if it was for something lovely like a turn on the bike.

Things came to a head when William was asked to come inside to a focus group one day and he responded very defiantly saying, 'No, I'm busy!' At that point an adult tried to take his hand and lead him inside which led to William lashing out and running away from her. We knew that things needed to change.

A colleague went on a behaviour course that discussed realistic expectations for children, and in particular boys like William. It was eye opening! We realised that we had nothing on offer in our setting to engage him and had developmentally inappropriate expectations for him. We were expecting him to sit still when his muscles were still developing and were asking him to draw or write before he was ready. No wonder he was rebelling.

We decided to change a few things, slowly at first, because change is difficult for staff as well as children. We removed waiting times, instead asking children to go and wash hands in twos or threes so that there was space for everyone at once. We also altered our routine with more continuous provision available inside and out and we stopped distinguishing between work and play – after all, children are learning loads through play. We enhanced some of these areas to try to encourage William to mark-make, rather than expecting him to come in and sit at a table. For example, we sourced an enormous cardboard box and left it outside with some crayons and found that he and some other children loved mark-making on all surfaces of the box. We left books about his favourite things (trucks and lorries) in the outdoor construction area with some clipboards with paper and pencils tied to them and found that William used them. Although we still plan some adult-led activities we do not force all children to participate in them. We also tried to limit our storytime to five minutes; if we're honest at times it had extended to over 20 minutes some days. William seemed to cope with this better and when he was asked to choose the book, although he still found it hard to sit still, he was jumping up and down through being so engaged, which was wonderful to see!

I am lucky to regularly visit schools and settings as part of my role, both as a university tutor and early years consultant. I meet a lot of children like William and see many situations that escalate when they do not need to. The expectations are not developmentally appropriate for all children and, just because a child may be capable of sitting still for a 20 minute storytime, it doesn't make it right or acceptable! Adults need to ensure that they have a full understanding of children and their needs and consider if they can change how they respond in order to make a positive difference. With a little more understanding, realistic expectations linked to developmentally appropriate practice and empathy from the adults, these children would be better supported and the low-level disruption avoided.

Avoid making assumptions

Linked with having developmentally appropriate expectations is the idea that we must avoid making assumptions when supporting children's behaviour and emotions. It is very easy to jump to conclusions about what happened or to think we know based on a child's past behaviour.

JUMPING TO CONCLUSIONS – A TEACHER'S PERSPECTIVE

Once when I had recently started teaching I went to a family party where there was a buffet table of food outside. As the table contained both sweet and savoury items, the children were asked to only take one muffin. I noticed my 4 year old nephew approach the table, look all around and then take three muffins and sneak away again. Thankfully I decided to watch rather than jump in and chastise immediately. He then ran over to where his brother and cousin were playing and gave them one muffin each. He was being really kind! This really highlighted for me the importance of not jumping in too soon with the children.

The case study demonstrates how easily adults can make assumptions. As we read the story, we are led to believe that he is taking three muffins for himself! Whereas actually he was behaving in a kind way that we should commend and celebrate. I once witnessed an occasion where children jumped to conclusions and made assumptions in a class when I was observing a student teacher. There was some sort of incident, I can't remember the details now, but when the teacher stopped the class and asked what had happened, she was told, 'Matthew did it!' and the teacher replied, 'Matthew isn't here today!' So the children had learned that if there were an incident, Matthew was often in the vicinity, and had put two and two together; however on this occasion, poor old Matthew wasn't even in school that day!

Sometimes what we say can lead to misunderstandings too. One child was told to draw the curtains in their childminder's home, who was horrified when he proceeded to get the crayons and colour in the curtains! We can easily assume that children understand what we mean, but sometimes what we say and what we mean are two different things. Research tells us that children in the early years age group do not understand metaphor, idioms and find figurative language difficult to comprehend. If we told a young child that time flies they might look out of the window, or if we say we'll get there in a minute, they might literally count to 60 and then ask why we're not there yet!

In her brilliant book, Fisher (2016) talks about the importance of educators standing back and observing and not being too ready to dive in and interact or even 'interfere'. She is mainly referring to our general practice, but I think the same is true of some more challenging behaviours we might observe.

Sharing

Sharing is an area where adults regularly have unrealistic expectations, so I want to explore this concept a little. As adults we rarely share with each other. We may occasionally share a pizza or bottle of wine with a friend, but we wouldn't dream of sharing our grown up toys, like our phone or our iPad, with others. Sharing does not mean the same thing to everyone and does not have the same implications in all circumstances. For example, if we share a train carriage with other passengers that has a very different meaning to how we might share a secret with our best friend. When we share a birthday cake with family, we need to cut it into slices and it is very different to sharing popcorn at the cinema with friends when we all dip our hands into the carton.

When we really start to reflect upon this, sharing is an abstract concept and more difficult to understand than we might originally think. Therefore it needs explanation, and one of the best ways to help children to understand this concept is to act as a role model and demonstrate what sharing looks like in practice. We can role model taking it in turns with others, labelling it as sharing and taking turns, and continually use the language associated with this. We can explain to children that we share in different ways, for example, sharing a slide may mean waiting our turn but sharing a packet of sweets could mean allowing everyone to have one sweet, and sharing a pizza means cutting it into slices so that we can all have some.

Developmentally children are beginning to understand the concept that some things might belong to me (mine) and some things belong to other people (yours). However, beginning to have this understanding is not the same as fully understanding. This is a concept that takes several years to develop because it relies upon children understanding the thoughts and feelings of others. This is linked to our development of Theory of Mind, which is explored later in this chapter, and most children under 5 have not developed this yet.

When we do see children sharing toys and resources with each other this is the ideal time to draw attention to it and use labelled praise, for example, 'Wow – I love the way that Jenna and Nazma are taking it in turns with the glue, great sharing!' For younger children it may be as simple as rolling a ball to a baby and saying, 'My turn, your turn…!' Sometimes we might want to plan specific activities which directly promote the skills involved with sharing, for example, turn-taking games, group activities or setting up a provocation where the children will need to share resources.

Sometimes challenges will arise and children may have arguments over toys and resources. This is the perfect opportunity to use the problem solving approach and emotion coaching techniques to help resolve the issues. Chapter 4 explains this in more detail. Most importantly, we need to have realistic expectations about our children: they may not yet be able to share, so we need to plan for this and accept it, whilst still actively promoting this skill and role modelling. In addition, we sometimes expect children to say sorry or apologise to one another. This is another example of an inappropriate expectation which is explored in detail in Chapter 7.

Theory of Mind

Children may be aware that other people have emotions, but young children cannot yet understand that they can influence these and that the feelings of others might be different to theirs. This is about their developing Theory of Mind and the ability to tune into the emotional states of others.

One of the ways that researchers determine if children have Theory of Mind is by doing a false belief test. Imagine you open your favourite box of chocolates to find that it has pencils inside. Your colleague comes in and looks at the box – what do they think will be inside? Chocolates? This is an example of a false belief, where someone believes something to be true that is not true because they do not have the same knowledge as you. When we do this test with a 3 year old, having shown them pencils in a chocolate box, and ask them what their friend thinks will be in the box, the child answers pencils because they have not developed their Theory of Mind yet. Most 5 year olds and all 6 year olds will answer chocolates because their Theory of Mind is developing. They understand that their friend has not yet looked in the box and thinks differently to them. Four year olds are in the middle with some who have developed Theory of Mind whilst others haven't yet. There are also groups of people who find this concept difficult, for example those with autistic spectrum condition (ASC), who are deaf or those with hearing loss or social communication difficulties.

Many of us may have developmentally inappropriate expectations as we assume our children will be able to empathise or understand how their actions and behaviour will impact others. We need to begin with the idea that our children may not yet understand and respond as we would to a much younger child. For example, if an 18 month old hits another child, we may say a clear, 'No!' and explain that we use gentle hands, but we would not chastise the child or hold them responsible for their actions in the same way that we would a 5 or 6 year old. We need to remember that some of our children under 5 are still developing Theory of Mind and do not yet understand that if they hit their friend it will hurt them. They are still learning the consequences of their actions and we need to respond more appropriately and actively seek to teach this concept, just as we would with a much younger child.

Children's Theory of Mind continues to develop in their primary school years. Some aspects of Theory of Mind develop much later, like an understanding of metaphor, figurative language, lies and sarcasm, as well as an awareness of faux-pas, which develops by around 11 years old. Some research suggests that Theory of Mind is still developing during adolescence into adulthood as we continually gain experience about how people act and react and develop our understanding of others (Meinhardt-Injac et al., 2020).

Empathy

Theory of Mind also has an impact on empathy and children's social competence because being able to imagine what another person feels like necessitates us to understand that others have their own feelings and thoughts to start with. Therefore this enables the child to be more sensitive to other people's thinking and helps them to manage these feelings and rely on non-verbal cues.

Most people define empathy in terms of placing themselves in someone else's shoes. This is a helpful way to think about this concept, however it is a very difficult concept for children to grasp and, as mentioned, is inseparably linked to Theory of Mind. I have sometimes heard people give the example of a baby crying in a baby room and another baby empathising and crying too. However, this is not true empathy. Does the baby understand that someone else is hurt or upset? No, they are going into survival mode and responding to the stimuli of hearing another infant cry, possibly thinking, 'Oh no, someone's upset, maybe I should cry too!'

Babies are social beings and learn a huge amount through imitation. We now know about the existence of mirror neurons in our brains which fire up when we see someone do something and we copy them, or when we do something and someone else imitates us (Ferrari & Rizzolatti, 2015). So in the baby room, the baby is connecting with the other baby on a neuron level and one is imitating the other and experiencing the same emotion. This is the foundation on which empathy is built as we start to experience the same feelings as others through mirroring them. However it takes many years for empathy to fully develop.

Therefore we can easily have unrealistic expectations of our children as we expect them to empathise with others. Instead, we need to accept that empathy is a skill that takes years to hone, and actively teach perspective-taking through role play, stories and talking about thoughts and feelings. We can also encourage children to be more emotionally literate by talking about feelings and emotions and what we do when we feel that way. We can share photographs of children feeling different emotions to help them identify and label their own feelings.

Sitting still

As educators we often expect young children to sit still for long amounts of time, mistakenly thinking that this will help them learn more effectively. This is inappropriate and research actually suggests the opposite is true. A report by the Institute of Medicine in the US found that 'Children who are more active show greater attention, have faster cognitive processing speed, and perform better on standardized academic tests than children who are less active' (2013, p. 2). Young children need time and space to develop their large muscles and children with low muscle tone will find it very difficult to sit for prolonged periods.

In addition to this, young children are still developing physically, in particular their vestibular (balance and coordination) and proprioceptive (awareness of where their bodies are around them) senses. This means they need plenty of opportunities to move and participate in active play throughout the day, and asking children to be sedentary for any length of time is unrealistic.

Many children will need to fiddle with things to help them concentrate, so rather than trying to prevent children from fiddling, we can actively support children's need for movement by keeping any sitting or sedentary times to a minimum, incorporating as much active movement into our routine as possible. During quieter times allowing the children to use fiddle toys or tactile toys, usually available from stores that sell sensory resources, will help them to focus. We can gather resources together in a sensory box containing a variety of different objects such as poppets, squishies, mirrors and fidget toys to help children to relax and focus their attention.

HAVING REALISTIC EXPECTATIONS – AN INTERNATIONAL SCHOOL EARLY YEARS TEACHER'S PERSPECTIVE

The longer I have taught, the more my expectations have developed to reflect what is appropriate for each individual child. I am fully aware the children I teach are very young, with the majority operating in a different language to their native language. Having researched child development I apply this knowledge in my setting. Therefore, when a child continues to play when they should tidy up, I simply remind them what we need to do. When they try to rush to be first, I applaud those that let their friend in front of them. I frequently discuss and praise kind acts and model them myself. If a child cannot sit or focus during adult-led activities, I let them move, have a look around, then draw them back in by my teaching. The better I know my children the easier this is to do – in fact, this is the key. If we have a clear understanding of children and accept them for who they are, we can provide them with realistic expectations.

Space

Another time when educators can have unrealistic expectations is over space. Children are expected to sit very close to each other and not touch each other. This is too big a temptation for many and an unfair expectation. So sitting children further apart, arranging them in a circle or arc, and using carpet squares or a rug with pictures on which define boundaries can help. As will clearing our rooms so that the optimum amount of space is available in the first place. If we identify a child who struggles with this more than others we can make extra space for them, sit them at the edge of the group or near an adult who can help to support them.

Making good choices

I often hear adults talking to children in terms of the choices they make, for example if an angry child hides under a table and the adult asks, 'Is that a good choice?' Framing behaviour in this way is not always developmentally appropriate because most young children will not have a full understanding of the situation and are still learning about right and wrong. Telling a child they have made a bad choice or asking a child if an action is a good choice is often meaningless. At that time, the child has wanted to act in that way and so for them it is a good choice! An example of this is a parent whose child takes some extra sweets from the sweetie jar. If the parent asks if that was a good choice, the child will undoubtedly think yes, I got some extra sweets! So we need to avoid talking in these terms with our preschool aged children because it is unhelpful and can even confuse them. Instead, we might talk to children about the bigger picture, other people's feelings and the consequences of actions.

As children grow older we can explain in more detail how some ways of behaviour may have different impacts and consequences and also link this with our own behaviour, however it is unrealistic to expect children under five to fully understand how to make a good choice. This skill will develop over time as they get more and more life experience and a greater under-standing about people and the world around them. We need to role model acting in acceptable ways and sometimes roleplay acting in inappropriate ways to spark discussion and get the children thinking. Speculating and wondering with the children can be a helpful way to get children engaged in this thought process.

WONDERING – A PRESCHOOL'S PERSPECTIVE

We always think that wondering is power in preschool. Asking open-ended questions or just commenting. I remember there was one little girl who was struggling to come into the setting one day. She had emotional issues and sensory needs and was outside with her father. I went and sat on the floor near her but not too close. I gently said, 'N you look so cross today. I wonder if you've had a bad morning… I've had an awful morning too!' I proceeded to tell a story about my morning and made it sound funny with all the many things that had gone wrong… N was listening and laughed at my story. I then added, 'I wonder how we can make it better? I wonder if you would like to come in and have a story?' N then happily came inside with me and we sat for a story together. I was able to say to her that we all feel upset or cross sometimes and acknowledge her feelings. If I had just said to her, 'Come on N, You'll be OK!' and tried to get her though the door, it would have ended badly and she would not have felt happy. As it turned out she felt that her feelings were validated and it resulted in her coming into the setting happily.

Wondering is when we think aloud so that the child hears and has the opportunity to respond. It is also a useful strategy if we are trying to connect with some harder to reach children. Sometimes it can be as simple as saying, 'I wonder if you are upset because Mummy has gone to work', whilst other times we might be speculating about something that has happened, 'I wonder if you really wanted to play with the red tractor that Jack has?' Keeping our comments speculative is helpful because we may not always be right. We might think we know how a child is feeling or what has happened but keeping our language tentative helps the child to know that we're not telling them how they are feeling or what happened, but are making a guess.

 **ACTIVITY**

Change these examples so that the expectations are more realistic and developmentally appropriate.

Inappropriate practice	Developmentally appropriate alternative which has realistic expectations
When an argument arises over a resource, children are told to share	
If one child has hurt the other, the instigator is made to apologise to the other child	
All 20 children line up together to wash hands before lunch	
When problems arise, the children know to ask an adult to solve the problem	
Children are allowed to play when they have finished all their work	
When a long story is chosen for storytime we manage to battle on to the end despite the children appearing restless	
When making Christmas cards the educators make an example for every child to follow and cut out the parts for easy assembly	
At the end of the Summer term there is a two hour graduation ceremony which children and families are invited to attend	
Throughout the year we plan our themes in advance so we have 'All about Me' in the Autumn, 'Growth' in the Spring and 'Seaside' in the Summer	

Concluding thoughts

It is vital that we have realistic expectations of our children otherwise we are setting them up to fail and fall short of our requirements. This necessitates us to have a really sound understanding of child development and age-related milestones. There are many common expectations that, when unpicked in the light of child development, are actually inappropriate, for example expecting children to share, say sorry or be empathetic. This chapter has explored these and many other areas offering an insight into what developmentally appropriate practices look like. The next chapter focuses on the powerful strategy of acknowledging and validating children's feelings.

QUESTIONS FOR REFLECTION

To what extent are our expectations developmentally appropriate?
Do all adults have a full understanding of each child, their strengths and their needs?
Are there any changes to the ways the adults respond that might make a positive difference?

 Further reading

The Birth to Five Matters Guidance document is very useful when considering child development and having developmentally appropriate expectations of our children. Find out more information at www.birthto5matters.org.uk/

Fisher, J. (2016) *Interacting or Interfering? Improving Interactions in the Early Years.* Maidenhead: Open University Press.

References

Ferrari, P. & Rizzolatti, G. (eds) (2015) *New Frontiers in Mirror Neurons Research.* London: Oxford University Press.

Fisher, J. (2016) *Interacting or Interfering? Improving Interactions in the Early Years.* Maidenhead: Open University Press.

Grimmer, T. (2021) *Developing a Loving Pedagogy in the Early Years: How Love Fits with Professional Practice.* London: Routledge.

Institute of Medicine (2013) *Report Brief – Educating the Student Body: Taking Physical Activity and Physical Education to School.* Retrieved from www.nap.edu/resource/18314/EducatingTheStudentBody_rb.pdf

Meinhardt-Injac, B., Daum, M. & Meinhardt, G. (2020) Theory of Mind development from adolescence to adulthood: Testing the two-component model. *British Journal of Developmental Psychology*, 38(2), 289–304.

Acknowledging and validating feelings

This chapter will draw upon research relating to emotion coaching and explain the importance of acknowledging and validating feelings. The key message is that all emotions and feelings are acceptable but not all behaviour. It will share useful phrases to use with children, examples and case studies of how to use an emotion coaching approach in practice and share the problem-solving technique for conflict resolution.

Introduction

Have you ever known someone *'make a mountain out of a molehill'*, when they disproportionately overreact to a situation? It is so easy to do, at home or even at work! For example, you pop into the staff room for a quick cuppa and notice that the cups haven't been washed… again! Last week you washed them all and over the weekend you made a laminated sign asking everyone to tidy up after themselves, but sadly this has been ignored and there is no clean cup for you to use!

At this point you have a choice about how to respond; you could make it VERY clear how unhappy you are and even refuse to go in the staff room in protest, or you could moan and grumble but not directly confront anyone. Perhaps you would decide that it's not worth the hassle and so you choose to ignore the cups and just wash one up for you to use. Alternatively, you could explain to your colleagues that you understand how busy everyone is and yet the staff room cups are getting you down so you want to find a way of sorting it so that everyone is happy and ask to spend a minute talking through some solutions in the next staff meeting.

DOI: 10.4324/9781003137474-5

Some of these responses would escalate the situation and possibly lead to more bad feeling, most would leave you feeling really bad and not resolve the issue, but the last option would acknowledge the feelings of all involved and, hopefully, lead to a resolution.

Emotion coaching

This example above is using an emotion coaching style of response which is based on the work of Gottman (Gottman and Declaire, 1997). An emotion coaching style considers the emotions that underpin behaviour and responds in the moment, acknowledges feelings and finds a way forward by setting limits and problem solving if appropriate. The key message is that all feelings and emotions are acceptable but how we behave in response to these feelings may not be (Digby et al., 2017), and that through their behaviour children are communicating their feelings with us.

Gottman's research was based around parents and the way they responded to their children (Gottman and Declaire, 1997). He found that parents tended to respond to their children in four distinct styles: disapproving, dismissive, laissez-faire and emotion coaching. He proposed that most parental responses do not take into account children's emotions, but using an emotion coaching style accepts all emotions as valid whilst at the same time acknowledging that how we behave as a result of having these emotions may need to be supported or discussed. For example, it's OK to feel cross when your brother takes a toy away from you, but it's not OK to hit your brother and snatch it back.

Although his research centred around parents and the home, we can use this approach in our settings too. An example I shared in my loving pedagogy book clearly explains these responses in the context of a child spilling a full cup of milk over a picture they have spent a long time drawing. 'Disapproving – Oh no – what did you think you were doing? I told you to move your picture before snack time. Dismissing – Don't worry about it – it doesn't matter. We don't cry over spilt milk. Laissez-faire – Sorry about that but I'm sure you'll manage to clean it up… Emotion coaching – You must feel really upset, you spent a long time drawing your picture. Let's find some paper towels and mop it up and then when it's dry we can colour it in together' (Grimmer, 2021).

Several of these responses are unhelpful to the child at that moment, but in using an emotion coaching response in this scenario, the adult offers both high levels of empathy and guidance so that the child has their feelings acknowledged and at the same time feels supported about what they need to do next. The last response, an example of emotion coaching, validates the child's feelings and offers them emotional and practical support. It does not take sides or apportion blame, instead it remains non-judgemental and practises acceptance of the children and their feelings. It follows three main steps:

1. Acknowledging and validating feelings, labelling them and empathising with everyone involved.
2. Talking through the situation, exploring the issue further and setting limits on behaviour if appropriate.
3. Resolving any conflicts, looking forward to the future and problem solving as necessary.

The first step is the most important – it is vital to acknowledge children's feelings and empathise with them. This in itself can begin to calm matters as children feel validated and better understood. We then need to explore the issue further by talking through the situation calmly. Our response should be empathetic while we try to understand what happened and why. We need to avoid taking sides and remain non-judgemental even if we initially think there is a child in the right and a child in the wrong. This is because we never truly see the whole picture. We cannot experience how another person feels and we must not make assumptions or value judgements about situations that arise. All the children involved have a right to feel the emotions that they feel regardless of how the problem arose or who started it. For example, it's quite normal and OK to feel jealous if I see my friend has a new handbag that I rather like, but it wouldn't be OK for me to take it from her! Having the feeling itself is understandable, it's what we do when we have those feelings that becomes right or wrong. So we are never thinking about the children as misbehaving, but rather thinking about their actions as misbehaviour.

The second step links with this when we might need to set limits on behaviour, so we could say that feeling envious of my friend's handbag is OK, but stealing it is most definitely not! This step helps to reinforce our boundaries and any rules that we may have in our setting and it is important to remain consistent with these. When all adults working with the children respond in the same way, children will learn about accepted behaviours more quickly because consistency of response reinforces children's understanding of what is right and wrong and why.

The last step in emotion coaching is not always needed in every scenario because it is about resolving any conflicts through problem solving. Sometimes the issue can be resolved through steps 1 and 2. However, there may be occasions when we need to turn challenging behaviour into a problem to be solved, and thinking about it in this way helps to keep our outlook more positive.

EMOTION COACHING – A RECEPTION TEACHER'S PERSPECTIVE

During the transition phase in September we visited the playground to show the children where they would be playing the next day after lunch. One child appeared to struggle with the idea of not being able to play right away. I enlisted my emotion coaching knowledge to acknowledge and validate his disappointment, saying, 'You really want to play on the playground now, it looks like lots of fun! You will definitely get to play on it tomorrow...' I also had to limit his behaviour by saying, 'I can't let you walk away, I have to keep you safe'. After being validated and giving time to process his feelings, he quickly calmed himself after his initial angry outburst and was happy to re-join the class. This interaction involved attunement with the child, listening sensitively and meeting his emotions with empathy and acceptance. This helped to contain his feelings through the process of co-regulation.

Problem solving

We often find children have disagreements in their play, and fights over toys and resources can easily arise. For example, in the sand pit, Celia and Emily begin playing well together until they decide to dig a really deep hole and then we find them arguing over the one big spade. The tug of war begins and eventually Emily says the worst insult anyone can think of… 'You're not coming to my birthday party!'

As educators we sometimes feel under pressure to rush in and sort out these arguments as soon as possible, or better still, attempt to stop them from happening in the first place by buying multiple sets of, well, let's face it, everything! However, little arguments and conflicts happen frequently and are a normal part of growing up. We need to allow children time and opportunities to resolve such issues themselves. In order for them to do this, we will need to role model and coach them through issues so that they learn how to respond when they have an argument or disagreement.

As a young teacher I came across High/Scope's wonderful six steps to conflict resolution which I highly recommend using and have employed successfully with children as young as 18 months old. I have since learned more about the High/Scope approach through 'Training as a Trainer' and would love to see a resurgence of this approach, in particular with settings adopting the problem-solving method, because this strategy really works with young children. So, let's think about Celia and Emily fighting over the spade and work through the six steps:

Step 1 Approach calmly

If we rushed over to the girls calling loudly, 'Celia, Emily, what's going on…?' we could make the problem worse. Rather approach calmly, using a gentle voice and get down to their level. Hold the spade but still allow Celia and Emily to hold it too. This will stop the tug-of-war whilst allowing both children to still feel that they have some control as they still hold part of the spade.

Step 2 Acknowledge children's feelings

Acknowledging feelings is a powerful way of demonstrating to children that you are open, actively listening and remaining non-judgemental. You may think you saw Celia take the spade from Emily, but try to remain neutral and open-minded, without allocating blame. Say, 'Celia, you look very upset' and 'Emily, you look very cross' – sometimes the mere fact that an adult is acknowledging feelings will calm things down very rapidly. This process also enables children to be more emotionally literate through labelling the emotions involved.

Step 3 Gather information

Ask the children what happened and describe the problem, or ask 'what?' questions to find out their view of what happened. Allow both children to speak. 'So, what happened?'

Step 4 Restate the problem

Again, try to remain neutral and matter-of-fact and repeat the information you have observed or heard. Check with the children that you have fully understood the issue.

'OK, so Emily was digging with the red spade and Celia really wanted the red spade so Celia took it from Emily. Is that what happened?' As you can imagine, they will soon tell you if you have got it wrong! Be prepared for the tug-of-war to begin again.

Step 5 Ask for ideas for solutions and choose one together

Tell the children, 'Celia and Emily, we have a problem! We have one red spade and... (counting) 1, 2 children who want to use it. What should we do?'

You will probably have a crowd of children around you by this point, as children love to watch other children fighting, or even better, getting told off! But no one is getting told off here and this can become a teachable moment for everyone, so ask your audience to help you with ideas. With very young children, or for the first few times of using this approach, you will need to role model by offering ideas for solutions yourself. Over time, children soon get the hang of it and will come up with all sorts of creative solutions to the problem.

Value all ideas that the children suggest and explain if they are not workable options. For example, if someone suggests they buy a new red spade, you may need to explain that you haven't got enough money to do that. Equally, they may come up with an idea that sounds good but won't work for these particular children; for example, Emily could have the blue spade and Celia could have the red spade. Emily may insist that she, too, wants the red spade so this won't work. At some point, the term share is usually banded about… It is important that you unpick this word as sharing means different things in different contexts. Celia and Emily choose to take it in turns to use the spade and to use the five minute sand timer to allocate time.

Step 6 Be prepared to give follow-up support

Start off Celia and Emily with the sand timer, ensuring that they are both happy with the solution. Tell them 'You solved the problem!' Then ensure that you are available when the sand has gone through the timer and the five minutes are up. Both children must get their turn or they will lose all faith in this process.

This strategy works really well and fits beautifully into an emotion coaching approach. There are many situations where following these six steps can resolve the issue calmly and amicably. It may even be worth printing them out and sticking them up on the wall for easy reference. When all adults in the setting work in this way with the children, role modelling potential solutions or ways in which the problem could be solved, children learn to adopt this approach themselves, and pretty soon you find that less adult intervention is needed as children independently resolve their own issues.

Here are some ideas for potential solutions when problem solving which we can share with children if they do not have any suggestions of their own. They will not all work in every situation so we may need to talk through how it may or may not work in this situation. I have made them into a set of problem-solving cards with words and pictures which children can flick through independently when problem solving without an adult.

- Take it in turns.
- Use a sand timer.
- Ignore.
- Say please.
- Play together.
- Swap.
- Wait.
- Use a promise card for older children (which states when child can play with the resource and all children sign).
- Purchase another resource or toy.
- Play with something else.
- Play with someone else.
- Ask a friend to help.
- Ask an adult to help.

De-escalation strategies

When dealing with children's emotions, how we respond, as the adult, will either make things worse and escalate the issue or it will defuse the situation and de-escalate matters. Problems will always get worse when the adult makes accusations or blames someone, uses intense body language and is unable to remain calm or shouts and raises their voice. Sometimes these ways of responding are very natural under the circumstances, however it is vital that we keep our own emotions in check when helping children to overcome theirs.

If we feel we are unable to remain calm, we are not the right person to support the child or group of children at that time and we need to remove ourselves from the situation so that we can calm down ourselves. This is why, if we work as part of a team, it is vital that we hold each other to account and support colleagues. If we work alone, we still need to allow ourselves time to calm down. When I was childminding alone, if I felt my own emotional barometer rising, I would make an excuse to go into the kitchen, or pop to the toilet, firstly checking that the children were all OK and no one was at risk of hurting themselves. However, as any parent of young children will know, sometimes even going to the toilet alone is a luxury we do not have on a daily basis, so we may need to find alternative ways of calming ourselves whilst still in the room with the children, for example by putting on some music. This can distract everyone and help to defuse things. We will also want to help calm the children down and Chapter 6 shares several calming strategies.

> ## EMOTION COACHING – A PRESCHOOL'S PERSPECTIVE
>
> We use emotion coaching to acknowledge and validate feelings, even for small issues. We ask children to come and have a chat, say we notice they look a bit cross / are struggling to listen etc. and wonder aloud why… Then we ask if there's anything we can do to make this better and help them. We use books about emotions at storytime and chat about them after we've read them. We use Theraplay (2021) group sessions to explore further (Theraplay is a therapy designed to support attachments, see https://theraplay.org/what-is-theraplay/). We have regular opportunities to discuss our emotions verbally and to recognise emotions in each other. We use 'wondering' to encourage the children to think of their own ideas and recognise their own feelings. For example, 'You look a little unsure today, perhaps you are feeling a bit unsure about leaving Mummy'. Then continue, 'I feel like that sometimes. I wonder if there's anything I could do to help… Is there something you'd like to play with first? Shall we go and get it out now?'

Using 'I' statements

Sometimes the way we word things can escalate or de-escalate the situation. For example, if I said to my colleague, 'You never wash up!' it is likely to make them feel cross. It is accusing them of 'never' washing up, which is not only untrue but an unhelpful thing to say. If I were to say, 'I feel as if I'm always washing up – the washing up is unending in this place!' The chances are my colleague would respond by grabbing a tea towel and saying, 'Let's do it together!' So using terms like 'you' and the language of blame, 'You never…', will always make things worse. Instead, changing the wording and putting the onus on us and how it makes us feel will shift the focus and make it more of a problem to resolve.

This is a great strategy when working with the children too; for example, if we see Kasper waving a stick around in the outside area, instead of telling Kasper, 'Stop waving that stick around, you're going to hurt someone in a minute…' we could say, 'Kasper, I'm worried that the stick will hurt someone'. Then go on to offer a practical way forward, 'You can either move onto the grass where there is more space, or use the stick differently keeping the end pointing downwards and away from your friends'. So changing the statement into an 'I' statement can help defuse the issue and turn it into a problem which can be solved.

These sorts of statements focus on the problem and the children's needs rather than seeing the child as the problem. They also remove the blame from a situation. It is really important that we have a no blame culture in our settings. That doesn't mean that we can't take responsibility for our actions but it does mean that we stop blaming and shaming people.

Focus on the present and future

The second part of the 'I' statement focuses on the future and gives a way forward for the child. When we focus on the past, like my example of saying my colleague 'Never washes up…' I am saying this *always* happens and not allowing for the idea that there may be times when they do wash up. This is about my mindset when I'm thinking about him and washing up. It is a very negative way to think and places the blame firmly on my colleague. We do this with children too, for example saying about a child, 'Sofia never sits still on the carpet…' We are again placing the blame on the child themselves and seeing them as the problem.

Instead we need to focus on the present and the future. In the present, 'Sofia is finding it difficult to sit on the carpet today', we offer Sofia a clean slate and can easily turn this into a problem, 'I wonder why Sofia is finding it difficult to sit on the carpet today…?' This has become a problem to solve and has shifted our focus into looking for solutions – perhaps Sofia is extra tired today or maybe she is not interested in what we're offering during carpet time?

Our children need to be loved, accepted and their feelings validated every day. We must ensure that we have wiped the slate clean for them every day and not dwell on the past, making assumptions about the future based on their past behaviour. Remember the story about Matthew in Chapter 3 – we must ensure that we're not jumping to conclusions about children or labelling them based on our past experiences.

Body language

You may have heard it said, 'A picture paints a thousand words' – so do our bodies: the visual image of our body language paints a thousand words to our children. I was once shown a series of photos of adults engaging with children. Some were pointing at the child, some standing over them in a threatening manner, some had a clenched fist, others had such an angry face you would think they had just been in a pub brawl. The adult was not touching the child in any of these pictures, however it was blatantly clear from the images that the adult was cross and the child was the subject of their anger. The images shocked me and also made me see how easily adults use their bigness and their idea of 'I'm the adult, you're the child, you do as I say…'

This is not right and has no place in civilized society. We should be protecting the most vulnerable and not using our power to dominate them. So we need to be very aware of the messages our body language is giving the children before we even open our mouths. Using intense body language, pointing fingers, clenched teeth or fists, bringing ourselves up to our full height… these are all strategies that we may employ to make us feel more powerful and strong. When we are with the children we must never act in this way. Instead we must use gentle body language and avoid using our bodies to display our strength. We are much taller than the children in our care. We can very easily intimidate and frighten them without trying to and introduce a power dynamic which is neither helpful nor necessary. So getting down to the children's level or lower is really important. This will particularly help children who are from homes where they have been bullied or bossed around and power dynamics are always in play. Our settings need to be counter to this and we should address the balance of power between the adult and child.

An emotionally literate setting

Working in the way described in this chapter and throughout the book could be described as being an emotionally literate setting. A place where we talk about feelings and emotions on a daily basis as part of our normal practice and routines. We can have emotions displays and read books and stories about emotions regularly. Children could make their own books too, for example a happy book, where they can draw or stick pictures in the book of things that make them happy.

Displaying photos or images of different emotions can also be helpful, if possible near a mirror and then we can pull funny faces in the mirror and encourage the children to make a happy face, or make an excited face or even an angry face... Many educators use puppets, soft toys or Persona Dolls to talk about emotions and use role play to explore different scenarios to discuss with the children.

EMOTIONAL LITERACY – AN INTERNATIONAL SCHOOL EARLY YEARS TEACHER'S PERSPECTIVE

In our school the majority of children do not speak English as their first language. Articulating about how they feel in a second language needs support. Often when children feel emotional, they will express this in their home language. We have bilingual learning assistants who can help and sometimes children translate for each other. However, we need to explicitly teach children about emotions and explain what might be seen as the basics. Prior to discussing this, we show pictures of faces and photos of different emotions, analysing together what the mouth and eyes look like to help children identify which facial expressions correlate with different emotions. We also discuss what our body does when we are emotional, e.g. fists clenched when angry or slumped shoulders when sad, and act these out together to further understand. After exploring several emotions in this way, the teacher role plays an emotion and sees if the children can identify it. After we have taught about a specific emotion, we add it to our wall display and the children can then match their face to the emotions and we discuss this. We use puppets and role play to help children understand what each emotion word means and how it makes you feel. We also have a hello song which sings through emotions and at the end we ask each other, 'How are you feeling?' We have noticed children using the pictures on the emotion wall to help express their feelings. As adults we need to be attuned to the children and respond sensitively.

 **ACTIVITY**

The examples below are of situations that can easily arise in our settings. How can you use an emotion coaching response to support these children?

Elijah

Elijah was carefully building with the blocks when another child accidentally knocked his creation over. Elijah shouted, 'Arghhhh' and kicked the blocks, then picked one up and threw it across the room. Luckily it didn't hit anyone.

Maisie and Liam

In the dressing up box there is one coveted superhero cape and several large pieces of material that children often use as capes. On one occasion Maisie and Liam are arguing over the cape and a tug of war has ensued.

Julie and Maia

Julie and Maia were playing Frozen in the home corner when Julie ran out crying. Maia called after her, 'You can't be Elsa anyway because I have long hair and you don't'.

Concluding thoughts

Emotion coaching and problem solving are powerful strategies to use and they work effectively because they validate everyone's feelings and accept all emotions whilst at the same time recognising our natural ways of responding and providing a calming way out. These approaches believe children to be competent and capable and support them to 'own' any problems, enabling them to become more independent and emotionally resilient in the future. In addition, because these approaches do not take sides, they can really defuse a situation and allow the molehill to be viewed as just that – a small molehill.

Emotion coaching relies on our being aware of emotions, tuning into our own feelings and those of our children, and sits within the context of a trusting relationship where we actively listen to children and value what they say and do. Chapter 5 explores how we can cater for the emotional needs of our children in our settings. So when we find ourselves responding emotionally to our children, colleagues, family and friends, let's remember to use an emotion coaching response. This will de-escalate the situation, acknowledge the feelings of all involved and resolve conflicts through problem solving. That way we won't make a mountain out of a molehill!

QUESTIONS FOR REFLECTION

In what ways do we validate and accept all children's emotions?
How can we ensure that we remain non-judgemental in our response?
How might we develop our use of emotion coaching techniques?

Further reading

Allingham, S. (2020) *Emotional Literacy in the Early Years: Helping Children Balance Body and Mind*. Salisbury: Practical Pre-School Books.

Find out more about emotion coaching at www.emotioncoachinguk .com/

References

Digby, R., West, E., Temple, S., McGuire-Snieckus, R., Vatmanides, O., Davey, A., Richardson, S., Rose, J. & Parker, R. (2017) *Somerset Emotion Coaching Project Evaluation Report: Phase Two.* Bath: Institute for Education, Bath Spa University.

Gottman, J. M. and Declaire, J. (1997) *Raising an Emotionally Intelligent Child: The Heart of Parenting.* New York: Fireside.

Grimmer, T. (2021) *Developing a Loving Pedagogy in the Early Years: How Love Fits with Professional Practice.* London: Routledge.

The Theraplay Institute (2021) *What is Theraplay?* Retrieved from https://theraplay.org/what-is-theraplay/

Becoming a behaviour detective

This chapter will share the importance of observation and getting to know our children really well. It will suggest that practitioners are very good at finding out children's interests but may not have considered this from an emotional perspective. It is as if we are behaviour detectives – we see the behaviour (a form of communication) but we need to unravel what the children are saying about how they feel and what they think through careful observation, listening to them and talking with parents and carers.

Introduction

We recently had a mystery in our house. I was clearing the draining board and putting the glasses away in the cupboard when I found a broken glass. A large piece of glass had snapped from one of my tumblers. I looked everywhere for the piece. I didn't want my family to tread on it. When I couldn't find it, I invited my family to help in the search and we all became detectives. We tried to remember the last time the glass had been used, looked on the drainer, opened cupboards, checked the dishwasher, we even looked under the fridge-freezer! This piece of glass had vanished! We had to admit defeat and stop looking – although one advantage from this was the kitchen was now the cleanest it had been in a long while! Even though we became detectives we were unable to solve the problem and locate the piece of glass.

Thinking about behaviour as communication is the most helpful way to support a child and ensure we respond appropriately. However, there is no magic wand for challenging behaviour. Sometimes we will

DOI: 10.4324/9781003137474-6

never know why a child behaves the way they do. We may never find that broken piece of glass or it may take a long time to solve the mystery. (We found it a few days later – it had fallen into an oven glove that was hanging from a cupboard below the worktop – you couldn't make this up!) Through reading this book we will not suddenly become experts and be able to calm and support the most difficult children we can imagine! However, hopefully we will seek to know our children better, to understand them more fully and to try to work out why they are behaving in this way. So this chapter is about becoming behaviour detectives!

Behaviour detectives

A detective is an investigator. Someone who gathers information to solve crimes or mysteries. Hopefully we do not have crimes to worry about in our settings, but we certainly have plenty of mysteries! How many times have we asked the question, 'Why?' in relation to children's behaviour? Why did he do that? Why did she say that? Why are all the boxes emptied out all over the floor? Why are the sinks blocked with green paper towels? Why are those children hiding under the slide?

All these questions and more provide us with pieces of the puzzle and in being a behaviour detective we are trying to find all these pieces and put them together, hopefully making them make sense. As with a jigsaw, we can sometimes see the bigger picture even if a few parts are missing, so although we will strive to find all the pieces, it is unlikely we will ever have them all. Despite this, we will work to put together as much of the puzzle as we can and draw upon our skills as detectives to gather information.

As early childhood educators we are really good at observing children and noticing who they play with, how they play and what might sustain their interest. We sometimes forget to use our observational skills to consider what children's behaviour is trying to tell us. As mentioned in the introduction to this book, it is my belief that young children do not want to misbehave – they actually want to feel loved, understood and accepted, so a large part of our role as an educator is to do just this. To love, understand and accept our children whilst helping them as they grow and develop.

It can be difficult to work out why a child behaves a certain way or what they are trying to communicate to us. I find it helpful to use the iceberg analogy explained in the introduction to help me unpick what is going on. So the behaviour that we see in terms of actions and words is just the tip of the iceberg and under the surface are the child's needs, reasons why they are behaving that way and what they are trying to tell us.

Questions we might like to ask in order to reflect upon the child and their behaviour include:

- Have their basic needs been met, e.g. is the child hungry or tired?
- What is the child trying to tell me?
- Is this child communicating something with us through the way they behave? (either consciously or not)
- Why do they do what they do?
- Could this behaviour be evidence of a schema (repetitive play)? (See Chapter 8)
- Could they be attention/attachment seeking?
- Does their emotional cup need refilling?
- Do they enjoy behaving that way?
- Do they like my response?
- Are they frustrated or feeling misunderstood?
- What is this child hoping to achieve through this behaviour?
- Has this behaviour been triggered by anything?
- What happened prior to this child behaving in this way?
- Has anything different happened at home?
- Is this behaviour a result of social interaction?
- Can we try to unpick why this child has acted or reacted in this way?

Given time we can probably think of more questions that would be helpful to ask. We then use our observations of how children behave in the same way that we would use our observations of their learning. We can reflect upon what the behaviour is telling us and then plan future provision and interventions in the light of this.

Knowing our children emotionally

Early years educators are really good at following the child and keeping their interests and needs central in our planning. We know when children are engaged and motivated, there is less time for poor behaviour. In following the child we get to know them really well and know even the smallest aspects of their lives, for example the names of their pets, their favourite PJ Masks character or where they went at the weekend. However, we also need to know our children's emotional needs really well. Then we can use all this knowledge to respond more sensitively to each child according to their needs and individual character. This will not mean treating all children the same because one child may need cuddles when they are upset or angry or worried, yet another may need to go and run or jump around in the outside area to release some of these feelings. When we know children really well, we will know which way to respond.

Here are a few questions that may help us get to know our children emotionally:

- How can we support this child and respond sensitively to their needs?
- What helps the child feel calm?
- What makes them excited?
- Do they have any objects or special toys that might help them to feel secure?
- What makes them anxious?
- When do they feel confident?
- Who do they feel most confident with?
- What are they frightened of?
- When might they feel cross?
- Which adult are they most securely attached to?
- When do they appear most at ease or comfortable?

Avoid making assumptions

It is easy to jump to conclusions and make assumptions when we consider children's behaviour. Chapter 3 has already explored this idea a little. Sadly, I have heard educators stereotype children in relation to their behaviour, naming children as a 'biter' for example. This is unhelpful and should be avoided. We might need to be aware that a certain child has bitten others, so that we can ensure we are closely observing, but our approach should be non-judgemental and every child deserves to have a clean sheet every day in terms of their behaviour.

For example, if we see Ahmed hit Josh, it would be easy to assume that Ahmed is angry with Josh and took his frustration out on him. However, this may not be true and we may have jumped to a conclusion here. Let's think this through with an analogy about a train which I am borrowing from my friend Kay Mathieson. I have observed that when lots of people appear on the platform (A) a train appears (B). We could imagine that A caused B or even that B caused A… but actually we know that neither of these statements are true. It is actually the fact that there is a train timetable (C) that caused both A and B. So the train timetable caused both the train to appear and the people to gather on the platform.

In becoming a behaviour detective we are observing a situation and trying to see if there are any other factors involved by viewing the behaviour as communication. So Ahmed hits Josh could be communicating a range of things from Ahmed's perspective:

- Josh is too close.
- I don't understand Josh.
- Josh doesn't understand me.
- I want Josh to play with me.
- I need a break.
- I'm overwhelmed.
- Josh hurt me.
- Josh always gets there before me.
- I need a friend.
- I want the toy Josh has and I don't know how to ask.
- I want to do this all by myself without Josh.
- I feel out of control.
- I'm tired or hungry.
- I need love.
- I need attention.

We could rewrite this list from Josh's perspective too. So instead of making assumptions, have a working hypothesis, and remain tentative in seeking to understand why a child has behaved the way they have. We must seek to learn more about a child and to scaffold their learning as they work out what others' actions and reactions might mean. Then we can explore possible ways of responding differently and hopefully support the child to communicate their needs more clearly and appropriately.

Listening to children

As a behaviour detective it is vital that we listen to children and try to find out their perspective. They are the reason we are being a detective in the first place! Everyone views the world from their own perspective, or through their own lenses if you like. It is very difficult to remove our own thinking and viewpoints which is why it is sometimes impossible to truly have empathy with others. We always have our own thoughts, opinions and starting point with regard to any issue. When we try to work out what children are thinking and feeling, it is important that we try to limit our lens and instead try to focus fully on the child.

An example of this is when different educators observe children and then discuss their observations. We have watched the same episode of play, however we will have picked up on different elements or made our own judgements about what was significant in this play. There is not always a right and wrong answer either; we may never fully know what is going on. One way to try to narrow this down is to talk to the children themselves.

So, depending on the age and stage of development, we can talk to the children and ask them what they think. Blank's levels of questioning states that children under 5 will find 'Why?' questions difficult (Blank et al., 1978) so quizzing a very young child about their behaviour may not get the desired response. Instead focus on simpler questions like, 'What happened?' or 'Who was with you?' Asking questions about perception are beyond the developmental ability of our children and can escalate the situation because asking why a child did something sounds very accusatory, so is best avoided. It is also important to remember that children sometimes say what they think the adult wants them to say.

Using a mosaic approach

If we are trying to find out what a younger child thinks we could adopt a mosaic approach (Clark & Moss, 2017) which attempts to view the world from the perspective of a child. It suggests we use a variety of methods to actively listen to children and through observation and child conferences try to build a 'A "living picture" of what being in this place is like' (Clark & Moss,

2017, p. 15). We then need to piece together the information, interpret and reflect upon it before translating it into action through changing aspects of our practice or providing continuity.

Hundred Languages of Children

This reminds me a little of the Hundred Languages of Children poem which expresses so eloquently the way that children have so many different ways of expressing themselves. For example, 'Children "write" in many ways, including movement, painting, sculpture, and computer animations' (Edwards et al., 2012, p. 7). It is the role of the educator to facilitate and enable the children to express themselves through the way they interact, set up the learning environment and provide open-ended learning opportunities. We can take inspiration from the Hundred Languages to help us piece together our behaviour investigation and remind ourselves that listening to young children and observing them involves a lot more than what they do and say.

Observation skills

We use the term 'attunement' when a practitioner, '…lets the child know his or her emotions are met with empathy, are accepted, and (if appropriate) reciprocated' (Rose & Rogers, 2012, p. 41). Being attuned to our children will enable us to truly observe.

Observation involves:

- Noticing – paying attention to where the child plays, what they do, how they do it and who they play with.
- Listening – listening to the interaction of the child with other adults and children, noting what they say, including tone, volume and body language.
- Reflecting – thinking about what we have seen and seeking to further understand the child. We may also want to consider the child's current level of development and the way the child is learning.

- Questioning – asking children questions in order to clarify, confirm or reject ideas about what we have observed.
- Recording – sometimes recording our observations – noting important features of the child's responses, behaviour, learning and development as soon as possible after observing them.

ABC / STAR analysis

If a child has a specific behaviour they repeat, we may want to explore why they behave in this way, for example if a child has begun hurting others. A useful tool to investigate this behaviour is to use an ABC or STAR analysis. These are ways of recording our observations which help us to unpick each incident and think about it in more detail. Then we can analyse the situation and look for patterns.

ABC stands for Antecedent, Behaviour and Consequences and we collect information under each heading:

Antecedent	Behaviour	Consequences
Where was the child? Who were they with? Explain the context in detail, e.g. time of day, part of routine etc.	What actually happened? What did the child do?	What happened next? How did the adult respond? How did any other children involved respond? What was the result?

A STAR analysis covers exactly the same ground in a slightly different format. STAR stands for Setting, Trigger, Action and Response:

Setting	Trigger	Action	Response
Where was the child? Time of day? Part of routine?	What happened? Can you guess why?	What did the child do?	What happened next? How did the adult respond? How did any other children involved respond? What was the result?

Sometimes when using an analysis like this we can ascertain why a child is behaving a certain way. Once we have gathered the information, we need to work out why the child is behaving this way. Are there any patterns in terms of day or time of day? Can we change the scene or context to prevent this happening in the first place? What exactly happened and compare this with what we want the child to do instead. Could anything about the situation be maintaining or rewarding the child for behaving in this way? Are they getting lots of 1:1 attention after the incident? Are there any other strategies we could use to encourage wanted behaviour instead?

One setting, on using an ABC analysis, noticed that one particular child was struggling on specific days of the week. With a little detective work they found out that this was when he had stayed at his dad's overnight. They were able to talk to his dad about this and it turned out that he had been having later nights and no routine due to staying up playing with older siblings which had been having an impact on his behaviour afterwards. They worked together with his father and encouraged him to follow a more consistent bedtime routine, with an earlier night, and this solved the problem.

ABC CHARTS – A NURSERY SENCO'S PERSPECTIVE

A child in our preschool room was struggling to engage and found it difficult to sit for any period of time. As SENCo I was asked to help. After discussions with his family and the room leader, we conducted an ABC chart and discovered it was only during circle/group times that his attention wandered. This made me reflect on the situation rather than suggesting the problem was with the child. I considered how we could help create a better environment and studied the routine of the classroom. After some deliberation I discovered children were being gathered in a group up to six times a day! The staff in the preschool room had become unaware of how much demand was being placed on their children and we quickly adapted the routine to provide more continuous provision and physical movement opportunities. We paired this with fiddle toys and gave the child his own 'carpet mat' to help him identify where he should sit. Whilst we didn't want to completely avoid group times as they did create some positive opportunities, we reduced them significantly and introduced new and exciting activities during these special times. This helped with the engagement of all children! Often, we can become 'stuck' in our own routines, and this can happen to even the best teachers! Continual reflection and open discussions with colleagues can help to identify simple changes which can make all the difference.

Teamwork

Detectives never work alone. They are always talking to others finding snippets of information here and there and trying to hold in mind their line of inquiry. So we must bear in mind the child we're investigating, so to speak, and talk to others about them. Firstly, discussing with the children to involve them in our thinking. Reflecting on learning and the way we behave jointly with children is an effective way of gathering the voice of the child. Using the mosaic approach and watching out for the Hundred Languages, but also sometimes talking directly with the children, bearing in mind Blank's levels of questioning to keep our discussion developmentally appropriate (Blank et al., 1978).

Secondly, we need to discuss with our own team of adults who work directly with the child. Everyone will have built a slightly different relationship and may have an alternative perspective about their behaviour. One of the strategies discussed in Chapter 6 is about consistency of response and how this is important. It is difficult to achieve this without teamwork.

RECAP TIME – A NURSERY TEACHER'S PERSPECTIVE

We use daily photos as well as adult observations taken from play. Educators skilfully talk about and unpick what has happened during group times, e.g. 'I could see Emily really thinking about how she could build her dinosaur house, and even when the logs wouldn't balance straight away Emily kept trying'. We use the characteristics of effective learning to help tailor the discussions. Educators recall instances where challenges occurred during the session, e.g. 'I could see Robin trying really hard to balance on the wooden logs outside', and we talk together about what happened next. Other children involved add in their own experiences, e.g. 'I let Robin hold my hand and we walked along the obstacle course together'. The educators help to extend the conversation further with the children, noting key emotions, e.g. 'What a reassuring and kind thing to do, thank you for holding Robin's hand, Robin gave such a big cheer and jump when she finished'. Then children often wish to share instances where they have helped others.

We reflect back on these key group discussions when challenges occur during the day as we can quickly remind children: 'Remember this morning when we talked about holding our friend's hands to help them balance, maybe you could do the same for Teddy?'

We also need to talk to the child's parents and carers and find out about their child from their perspective. Many children behave differently at home so we may add a few more pieces of the puzzle by listening carefully to what parents and carers have to say. We can try to find out more about their lives, where they go, what activities they might do on certain days after leaving our setting etc. as this information helps us to think about the child holistically. We may also need to be part of an extended team of people if the child has additional needs, medical needs or if our setting is struggling to support them without outside help. Multi-agency and inter-professional working is when professionals and different organisations work together to discuss and support the child, often in a 'Team Around the Child'. The sort of people involved could range from health professionals like a physiotherapist, speech and language therapist or occupational therapist, to local authority or borough inclusion officers.

Using this information

Once we have gathered the information, we need to use it to help resolve things for the child and act upon our findings. There are many ways we can do this as the list below shows:

- tapping into children's interests
- planning activities/experiences to extend and support learning and development
- supporting the child in the moment through sensitive interaction
- changing our routine to support the needs of the child
- changing the layout of our learning environment
- sharing what we have observed with others (parents, outside agencies).

When we know our children really well we can easily tap into their interests and use this as we plan our provision. When children are highly engaged and have intrinsic motivation to join in with activities or resources, there is less time for poor behaviour. Sometimes certain behaviours are simply because a child is bored or not interested in what we are providing for them. For example, we know that a child who often flits from activity to activity like a whirlwind has a pet dog, Benji, and she recently told us that she took Benji to the pet doctor. We might decide to set up a role play scenario as a vets, include some books about dogs or with characters as dogs in our book corner and ensure that resources and props such as soft toy dogs, dog bed, dog toys and collars are freely available. We could even arrange a visit to our local vet or pet centre.

Our observations may also help us to plan activities and experiences which extend and support learning and development. For example, we observe that a younger child is very interested in enclosing and containing, so we provide additional resources and materials to encourage this schema, like different sized boxes and containers with lids, as well as large pieces of paper and material which they can use to wrap themselves.

When we consider our findings, we will hopefully better understand how to support the child in the moment and interact more sensitively with them. Fisher talks about *maintaining the learning momentum* through commenting, pondering, imagining, connecting, thinking aloud, talking about feelings, reflecting back to children, supporting the child to make choices and decisions, explaining and informing, posing problems and sometimes through staying quiet (Fisher, 2016). This links with *sustained shared thinking* (SST) when an adult is tuning in, showing interest, elaborating, re-capping, offering own experience, clarifying ideas, suggesting, reminding, encouraging, offering an alternative viewpoint, speculating, reciprocating, asking open questions and modelling thinking (Siraj-Blatchford, 2005). When we interact in this way we pick up on the teachable moments that present themselves during the day, we remain attuned to the children and we maintain children's interest and attention, again meaning they are more likely to behave in acceptable ways.

Sometimes our investigations may lead us to change our routine to better support the needs of the child. For example, if we notice a child is very irritable first thing in the morning, we may decide they are getting 'hangry', hungry and angry! So we try moving our snack earlier or introduce a rolling snack bar and then observe again and see if this solves the problem. Perhaps we have noticed that late morning our group of 2 year olds are getting very tired and clingy, so we introduce a quiet time immediately after snack time when everyone settles down to nap, read or just play quietly indoors rather than move straight from snack to another busy activity or experience.

We may find we want to change the layout of our learning environment as a result of our detective work, for example we may have noticed a child frequently running inside. So we move the furniture to break up the room in such a way that it discourages running and encourages more sustained interaction and we ensure there are plenty of opportunities to run outside. Or we may notice that several incidents have happened in a part of our outside area difficult to see because of the location of our outdoor storage, so we move the storage containers which allows us to supervise all areas again and reduces the number of incidents.

As a first step, we will often choose to have an informal chat with the child's carer to check that everything is OK at home. Sometimes this sheds light onto the situation, for example we may find they have had a couple of really late nights which might explain the behaviour. We may need to share what we have observed more formally with others. This will still include the child's parents and carers but may also include any other agencies or professionals involved with the child and family. We may occasionally have concerns from our observations and want to share them with an outside agency – whenever possible, we must seek parental permission for this, unless we believe that in doing so we would put the child at further risk. We might be concerned about the development of a child's speech and language and we may like to encourage the parent to talk to their health visitor or refer the child to a specific service.

Sometimes our investigations suggest we should observe the child further to gather more information. The aim is to try to notice any patterns in their behaviour which will help us to unpick what is going on. We may decide to focus our observations on a specific aspect, time of day or area of our provision. This may add detail to our picture of the child's behaviour and help us understand what they are communicating through behaving in this way.

ACTIVITY

Think about one child in your setting whose behaviour you struggle to understand and support. Become a behaviour detective and try to unpick the situation further, thinking in more detail about why this child may be behaving in this way. To help achieve this you may like to draw an outline of an iceberg and write their behaviours, what you actually see and observe, above the water level. Then consider what might be underpinning this and write these ideas under the water level. You may like to use the list of questions earlier in this chapter to help analyse their behaviour. Remember to note any emotions involved.

Concluding thoughts

As behaviour detectives we are continually seeking to find out more about our children and why they behave the way they do. We are asking ourselves what they are trying to communicate with us and then reflecting upon this to change or adjust our practice in the light of our investigations. Knowing how children respond emotionally will help us in this task. By listening to children, closely observing them and being attuned to their needs and individual personalities, we will begin to see the bigger picture and learn how to respond appropriately to our children. Chapter 6 explores this response and shares many strategies we can adopt.

QUESTIONS FOR REFLECTION

To what extent do we know each of our children emotionally?

How does our learning environment support children's emotional development?

Is there anyone we need to share our observations with? In or out of the setting?

Further reading

Clark, A. & Moss, P. (2017) *Listening to Young Children: A Guide to Understanding and Using the Mosaic Approach*. London: Jessica Kingsley Publishers.

Edwards, C., Gandini, L. & Forman, G. (2012) *The Hundred Languages of Children: The Reggio Emilia Experience in Transformation*, 3rd edn. Westport, CA: Praeger.

Mainstone-Cotton, S. (2019) *Listening to Young Children in Early Years Settings: A Practical Guide*. London: Jessica Kingsley Publishers.

References

Blank, M., Rose, S. & Berlin, L. (1978) *The Language of Learning: The Preschool Years*. New York: Grune & Stratton.

Clark, A. & Moss, P. (2017) *Listening to Young Children: A Guide to Understanding and Using the Mosaic Approach*. London: Jessica Kingsley Publishers.

Edwards, C., Gandini, L. & Forman, G. (2012) *The Hundred Languages of Children: The Reggio Emilia Experience in Transformation*, 3rd edn. Westport, CA: Praeger.

Fisher, J. (2016) *Interacting or Interfering? Improving Interactions in the Early Years*. Maidenhead: Open University Press.

Rose, J. & Rogers, S. (2012) *The Role of the Adult in Early Years Settings*. Maidenhead: Open University Press.

Siraj-Blatchford, I. (2005) Quality interactions in the early years. Paper presented at TACTYC Annual Conference Birth to Eight Matters! Seeking Seamlessness – Continuity? Integration? Creativity? Cardiff, 4–5 November.

6 Strategies to support challenging behaviour

This chapter will explore some specific strategies employed to support children when they behave in challenging ways and will cross reference many of the other chapters in the book. The key message is that our response should be non-judgemental and there is no sliding scale relating to poor behaviour, instead there are children who are feeling big feelings and have not yet learned how to cope with them.

Introduction

Strategies to support children's challenging behaviour are rather like tools in a toolbox. When we are using tools, we tend to select the most appropriate one for the purpose. Sometimes we don't know which size screwdriver we need, so we might try a couple. The same is true of our behaviour strategies, we need to respond using the best strategy for that moment and may try a couple of different techniques when dealing with challenging behaviour so it is useful to have as many tools in our toolbox as possible. This chapter shares some key strategies and when we might need to use them.

Responding positively

Part of our positive response is to tap into children's intrinsic motivation. We need to tap into children's interests to encourage this because

DOI: 10.4324/9781003137474-7

where children are engrossed and have high levels of involvement there is less time and opportunity for misbehaviour!

Here is a list of positive ways of responding which we should bear in mind when supporting children:

- Stay calm, keep voice calm and quiet and choose words carefully.
- Get down on child's level or lower and avoid imposing body language.
- Acknowledge feelings.
- Offer consistent approach.
- Use positive labelled praise, e.g. 'Great turn-taking guys!'
- Role model feelings.
- Include calm down time/space in daily routine.
- Turn incidents into opportunities to learn.
- Respond mindfully rather than reacting emotionally.

Remaining calm is vital if we are to support children with their behaviour. If we lose control or get angry, we will not be in a position to act as a co-regulator for the child. Sometimes we become good actors as educators, however our body language and tone of voice can easily give our feelings away, so we must ensure we keep our voices calm and quiet and use gentle body language. Getting down on the children's level or lower also helps to remove the power dynamic as mentioned in Chapter 4. We are big and they are small and it is very easy for young children to feel frightened and intimidated by us.

In addition we should choose our words carefully. Asking a child, 'What are you doing?' or 'Why are you doing that?' can be accusatory and sound like an interrogation which is unhelpful. Instead, using 'I' statements (see Chapter 4) or wondering are more productive and remove the unintentional demands. Some children find requests and demands placed upon them very difficult to manage. If we notice this is the case, we can rephrase things to make them less demanding. For example, if we want a child to put on their wellies and we think they will object we can say, 'When you have your wellies on we can jump in some puddles'.

As mentioned in Chapter 4, acknowledging feelings is a powerful strategy and should be part of our everyday practice with children. We also need to offer a consistent approach, so that all adults working with the children respond in the same way. This helps children to know where they stand and avoids the temptation of their playing one adult off against another, which can happen if a child realises that one adult may say no but another adult may say yes! Chapter 9 considers how we can aim for a consistent approach with parents and carers too.

Another strategy to continually use is positive labelled praise and encouragement when we state what we are celebrating or the behaviour we want to encourage, for example, 'Harry I loved seeing you use kind hands with Kyle earlier in the mud kitchen!' Praise can come with a judgement; for example, although saying, 'Good boy, you've made a great tower!' sounds effective, it is giving the subtle message that it is only because he made the great tower that he is good. What if his tower wasn't quite as great, would he still be good? Encouragement is non-judgemental, so we can say something like, 'You must be so proud of your tower!' or 'You worked so hard in building your tower today' which gives the message that the child should feel proud of themselves and their hard work was the important thing, not how great the tower is. So labelled praise or encouraging statements can work very effectively; for example, 'Sara you are listening really carefully!' This type of statement helps children to feel good, but focuses on effort and not attainment.

We can also role model feelings ourselves and include the language of emotion in our everyday speech, for example, 'I'm really excited because my daughter has her birthday this weekend!' or 'I'm a bit worried that the book I ordered online will not arrive in time for me to wrap it!' There are some lovely books about feelings that we can use with the children and sometimes creating scenarios using puppets or toys can be a really powerful way of explaining which emotions are which and how we should and can respond when we feel that way. So we can set up scenarios where we 'spill the milk' and then show our resilience in cleaning it up. Some children will be coming from homes where spilling the milk gets a very negative response – again, we need our schools and settings to counter this and give a clear message to children that it's OK to make mistakes, we all do, and this is how we deal with them. Children will often imitate behaviour, so give them something positive to copy and be an effective role model.

We also need to ensure that we have places where children can go if they need to calm down and include quieter times in our routine so that the whole day is not too full on. Everyone needs some rest and relaxation time, even if only for a few minutes. Allowing children places to escape can add to their feelings of safety and security as Chapter 1 explores. We can include a sensory bag or calm-down box as part of our continuous provision which includes resources such as mirrors to see our facial expressions, picture books about feelings, fiddle toys and soft cuddlies.

Another positive way of responding to incidents is to see them as opportunities to learn about what to do when we are overwhelmed and how to respond mindfully rather than react emotionally. We can also use emotion coaching techniques with children and problem solve discussing and resolving real issues with the group. This may involve explicitly teaching children strategies to use independently, for example conflict resolution, mindfulness, grounding, breathing and calming techniques. Our aim is to develop skills in the children so that they can independently resolve future conflicts.

It is important to give children lots of reassurance, love and build up their self-esteem, ensuring that they know there are things they do that we like or dislike but we still love and respect them regardless of their behaviour.

Setting rules

It is really helpful to have clear expectations and share them with our children, perhaps in the form of some basic rules. Depending on the age/stage of the children we support, we may be able to devise these rules with them. Our rules need to be written as simply as possible and in a positive way, for example rather than, 'No running' we would say, 'Please walk'. Rules also need to be understood by all, so if a setting caters for children aged from birth to 5 years, the rules in the toddler room may read more simply than the rules in the preschool room. We need to reinforce our ground rules in context regularly throughout the day as and when the opportunity arises. Having rules also helps adults to remain consistent in their response to children.

Another reason why it is important to present our rules positively is that we tend to hear the last thing that has been said. So if I say, 'Do not hit' the part of this sentence we hear is 'hit' and that almost becomes an instruction! If I say, 'Have kind hands' this problem does not arise. When we use terms like 'kind' or 'share' with our children, we must also unpick what they mean because these terms are quite abstract without explanation. Chapter 3 explores this idea around sharing in more detail.

> ## OUR CLASS RULES – A RECEPTION TEACHER'S PERSPECTIVE
>
> At the beginning of the school year Rabbit Class set their own rules. I have found children are more likely to remember and understand the rules if they have some ownership of them. So during one of our first circle times, we create some rules together. Usually the children come up with initially quite a negative list of behaviours to avoid, for example no hitting, no spitting, no kicking etc. Then we discuss this and try to write it down in a positive way, e.g. we are always kind to our friends. If I need to, I share some different scenarios with the children in order to scaffold their thinking and ensure our rules cover all bases. I scribe as the children talk and model writing as we create a display usually entitled 'Rabbits' Golden Rules'. We display them in the cloakroom area which people walk through to get into our room.

Calming techniques

Challenges often arise when emotions run high. Knowing how to de-escalate the situation and calm things down is essential. There are a number of different techniques we can use to help children to calm down. As Chapter 5 explains, it is vital to get to know our children really well so we can work out which child needs to run around outside and which child needs a cuddle to help them feel calm.

We also need to build calming activities and exercises into our daily routine. There are lots of ideas in this chapter, but the most powerful strategy is to acknowledge feelings and name them which Chapter 4 has discussed. Young children often have big feelings and emotions that they don't know how to handle. If we can name them for the children, it gives the feeling a label and validates and accepts the feeling. For example, 'You look very cross… When I feel cross I stamp my feet' or 'You sound really excited… Feeling excited makes me want to jump up and down!' This can help the child to understand which is which and what to do when they feel that way.

Routinely responding in a manner that validates feelings and using an emotion coaching approach will help to de-escalate situations as they arise. Sometimes we will also need to use specific calming strategies for an individual child in the moment and at other times we may want to directly teach children calming techniques. Here are some ideas to try:

- Counting games – counting is great because it literally gives us time to calm down and focus on something.
- Breathing exercises – when we breathe deeply and evenly we get more oxygen to our brain which helps the upstairs brain to take over again. Lovely exercises include pretending to blow out the candles on a birthday cake, blowing up a pretend balloon, or going outside on a cold day and making dragon breath.
- Songs or rhymes – the more involved a child can be with these the faster they will calm down. They act as a distraction technique, and because singing requires us to breathe regularly it has the same effect as breathing exercises.
- Rhythmic actions – for example, action rhymes, marching, swinging arms, stretching or rocking a baby. Again, this usually helps to regulate our breathing and heart rate too.
- Music – this can have a very calming effect on a whole group. One idea is to lie down on our back, close our eyes and listen to the music, or give the children ribbons and scarves and ask them to move; with calm music they tend to sway and make elaborate arm movements rather than excitedly jump about.
- Pressing on shoulders or bear hugs – these strategies rely on educators knowing their children really well, which means first talking to parents about any physical strategies they use that calm their children. Some children love to have a shoulder rub/massage or their shoulders pressed down firmly, whilst others may need a tight embrace to help calm them. We can also include massage in circle time for example, encouraging them to massage hand lotion into each other's hands.
- Sensory activities – using our senses can also distract us and have a naturally calming effect, for example using lavender scented play dough, or teaching children a simple grounding technique which asks them to focus on five things they can see, four things they can touch, three things they can hear, two things they can smell and one thing they can taste.

- Emotionally literate environment – this is part of having a calm routine, using photos of emotions and reading books that talk about our feelings etc.
- Worry dolls and worry monsters – the idea here is 'a problem shared is a problem halved' as these dolls or monsters encourage us to tell someone about our worries. They can be part of our routine and children can learn to post their picture into the monster's mouth, or even write their worry if they are able, and this acts as a prompt for educators to respond to this child.
- Yoga and mindfulness – again we can include these activities as part of our routine and children can learn some simple meditations and yoga moves that they can then use when they need to calm down in the future.
- Calming resources – we can use bubble tubes or lava lamps or create calming bottles where we mix some coloured water and oil and as they settle the children can watch them separate. Liquid timers are also calming to watch and a useful addition to our settings.
- Safe spaces – offering the children places in the setting where they can snuggle up, hide or just relax also gives them places to escape to if they need to calm down.
- Dim lights, limit noise in the room – this can immediately have a calming effect on the whole group.

Ignoring

Ignoring is a useful strategy to use sometimes. The phrase 'Turn a blind eye' comes to mind here, because sometimes we need to ignore the behaviour and the child will stop. This can work well if it is low-level disruption, for example, if a child is making an annoying noise and it appears they are attention seeking. We can ignore the noise and instead of addressing it we can offer the child an alternative activity which gives them the attention they desire. The disruptive noise will usually stop.

Ignoring can also work if we have more than one behaviour to address because we cannot tackle everything at once. We need to prioritise and concentrate on the most challenging or any dangerous behaviour first. So if a child is using their fingers instead of trying to use their cutlery, but also rocking on their chair, we want to address both, but this will probably be received badly and sound like a telling off, and the rocking on the chair is potentially dangerous, so we 'turn a blind eye' to the lack of cutlery use and gently remind them to keep all four legs of the chair on the ground. Remember to use an 'I' statement: 'I'm worried the chair might fall back-wards and you would get hurt'.

Distraction

Distraction is also a useful strategy and works best for younger children. This is when we ignore the behaviour we want to tackle by redirecting the child's attention elsewhere at something totally unrelated to the issue… 'Oh look, is that a helicopter?' or 'I wonder what we're having for lunch?' or 'Look, here's your favourite book, shall we look at it together?' Distraction can also work by setting up and playing with an alternate activity in sight of the child and making it very attractive and fun. This new activity can distract the child away from a different area or the behaviour they were displaying.

Using signs and gestures

Several behavioural challenges arise out of feelings of frustration or a desire by a child to feel better understood. One useful strategy is to use sign lan-guage and gestures to aid communication. Research shows that babies and young children who sign communicate with others much earlier than their non-signing peers and using sign language decreases the frustration that chil-dren can feel at this age (Acredolo & Goodwyn, 2009). Many educators are choosing to enhance their communication by using gestures and signs and this is now considered to be effective inclusive practice with benefits for both children and educators.

ABC or STAR analysis

ABC and STAR analyses can help us to unpick why a child behaves in a certain way and are explored in Chapter 5. Having strategies like this up our sleeve is really helpful and offers us more tools for our toolbox.

BEHAVIOUR STRATEGIES – AN INTERNATIONAL SCHOOL EARLY YEARS TEACHER'S PERSPECTIVE

When I perceive a child is struggling with self-regulation, I watch for the antecedents or triggers for certain repeated behaviour to try to unravel what has happened and how the children feel. I have noticed that often children do not yet have the problem-solving skills of what to do should there be an issue with sharing. In this situation I present the issue back to them. If they cannot think of how to resolve it, I reflect with them on systems we have in our class that support decision making. In one incident, the child thought for a moment, then requested a sand timer. The child then decided at the end of the timed five minutes the item would be swapped over. This was agreed with the other child concerned. The timer was carried to other areas of the provision and the children had a good understanding and all began to use it. Later in the year, we introduced 'Stone, Paper, Scissors' to continue to support decision making.

Common behaviours and ideas of how to deal with this behaviour

This next section will unpick some common behaviours we may struggle with and offer ideas and strategies of how to deal with this. The ideas I am sharing are only suggestions and knowing the children really well will help us to recognise if these strategies will work in each scenario. If they do not work, we can try other tools from our toolbox.

Attention-/attachment-seeking behaviour

As Chapter 2 suggested we need to think about this as attachment-seeking behaviour and find ways of filling children's emotional cups, giving them as much attention as possible when they are behaving appropriately. If they are displaying attachment-seeking behaviour, calmly ask them to stop, for example, 'If you stop XXX we can go and play a game together', which will give them attention when they stop this behaviour. If they are seeking our attention when we are busy we need to explain to the child why we are unable to come or help them now and offer them attention as soon as possible, for example, 'I will come and look as soon as I have finished changing this nappy'. If possible we can also involve the child in what we are doing while they are waiting, for example, 'Can you pass me the baby wipes?'

Fussy eaters

We must check with parents and carers that the child does not have any issues regarding oral health, for example, tooth cavities, muscles in mouth that find it hard to chew, or any pain or discomfort when eating, and double check for any allergies. Be a detective and try to work out why they are being fussy. Is it the texture, smell or taste that is being rejected? We can find out from home what their favourite foods are and incorporate these into our menus. We also need to check portion size; perhaps we are serving too large a portion for their age? Sometimes fussiness over food is about control, however we must avoid power struggles at the table (or anywhere) – instead we can encourage healthy choices and create a table rule, for example, that we taste everything on our plate. Ensure that we sit with the children and eat the same food together and keep presenting unwanted foods over a period of time, without any pressure to eat it all.

Tantrums

It is vital that we remain calm ourselves when dealing with tantrums. We also need to distinguish between a true 'tantrum' and an attachment-seeking episode. During a true tantrum the child is in freeze, fight or flight mode and they need to calm down. We must make sure they are safe, only moving them if they can hurt themselves, then wait. Singing songs, rhymes and doing actions or marching using a rhythm may help them to calm down. Once they are calm, we will need to refill their emotional cup so hug or comfort them and acknowledge they felt really strongly about the issue. If this is attachment-seeking behaviour, the child will probably quieten then look up to check if we are still watching and when they have our attention begin to scream again. This is not a true tantrum and we need to find ways of offering this child plenty of attention on our terms when they are calm. Ignoring the screaming and playing with something they love nearby can entice them out of the cycle. Show them there is space beside you for them to play. Acknowledge their feelings, saying, 'I can see that you are upset and it's OK to feel upset. It's not OK to scream when you are upset'. Then spend some time with them on their favourite activity. Over time they learn that they receive the attention when they are calm, not when they scream.

We must learn to read the signals of our children, pre-empt triggers and avoid them. We can also use a STAR or ABC analysis to try to work out why the tantrums occur. Then address our findings, for example if we felt the child was frustrated at not being understood, we would use sign language and lots of pictures alongside words to help develop their communication, be patient and allow them time to get their message across. We also need to know how best to calm our children so that we respond appropriately by cuddling or allowing them to run around to let off steam.

Screaming/whining

When a child is screaming, replying in a really quiet voice or in whispers usually lowers the volume. The child needs to quieten to hear what we are saying. Having a general rule about using inside voices and offering lots of opportunities for outdoor play where children can shout and scream if they want to can help. We can also use sign language to alleviate frustration, teach alternatives to screaming such as jumping on the spot, running around outside or 'silent-screaming' when we feel like screaming. Role modelling using a quiet voice and gentle tone can also help. Try to ignore whining to show children that whining will not achieve anything. Remain calm and give positive attention when they stop whining. We can also empathise if they are unable to do something, for example, 'I'm sad that we can't stay any longer too…'

Inappropriate language

Sometimes when children use inappropriate language the temptation is for us to laugh and share with our colleagues what the child has said. Avoid doing this as it can make the child want to repeat the word or phrase for entertainment value. If possible, ignore the language if it is a one-off and repeat back the sentence replacing the inappropriate word with an appropriate one. If the language is repeated we need to explain to the child that we don't use those words or that is not a kind thing to say and provide an alternative positive thing to say instead, ensuring that we role model appropriate language at all times.

Lying

Research tells us that lie telling is common in young children and is a result of both cognitive and social factors (Nagar et al., 2019). However, young children do not fully understand that lying is wrong and sometimes they truly believe what they are saying, so do not worry if young children tell lies. We can ask them, 'Is that really what happened or do you wish that happened?' and explain that telling the truth is important, using labelled praise when we notice them telling the truth. Sometimes children say things that are untrue for attention or to avoid being told off, so our response is important. Bear in mind what we have thought about in relation to children developing Theory of Mind because this is closely linked with children's ability to tell lies (Lavoie et al., 2017). Therefore we need to consider children developmentally and tackle any lie telling according to their age and stage of development.

Hurtful behaviour

Many educators find hurtful behaviour the most difficult to deal with. Children can hit, kick, bite, push and hurt others in many different ways. It is really important that we maintain a 'no blame' culture. The first thing we need to do is say to the child, 'Stop!' with a clear gesture. If they are bit-ing we can offer sensory activities, teething rings, have fruit freely available and share stories about not biting others. Other ways to respond to hurtful behaviour include using sign language, having as high a staff:child ratio as possible, using picture cues, maintaining a consistent approach and teaching about empathy and feelings. We can also use labelled praise when children use words instead of hurtful behaviour, for example, 'Kazia, I'm so pleased you used your words today when you felt really cross with Zac...'

Finding sharing difficult

Chapter 3 has explored what to do when children find sharing difficult. The key message here is that sharing is an abstract concept and young children will not share so we must adjust our expectations and deal with it, whilst teaching the skills and language associated with sharing.

Defiance or disrespectful behaviour

Many adults find they are rattled by this behaviour, so again, we must keep our own emotions in check when we deal with this. Our detective skills are needed as we try to work out why the child said no or was disrespectful. Offering time warnings prior to transitions can help children to know they will have to stop playing or tidy and it can also help to prevent any defiance caused by their desire to keep playing. If they are being disrespectful, they may need positive attention and might not fully understand that what they have said is disrespectful. For example, a young child may say, 'You are fat!' and not realise this is inappropriate. Or they may argue with an adult or answer back without realising that social etiquette means they should not. Again, this is related to Theory of Mind or rather the lack of it! We must role model respectful actions and words, use labelled praise when children comply or are respectful and use 'I' statements, telling them how we feel. 'I felt very sad when you stuck your tongue out at me, how can you help me to feel happy?' It is important not to take anything a child says personally, bearing in mind that they do not yet fully understand what they are saying or the implications of their behaviour.

Destructive behaviour

Sometimes children might tear up books, knock down towers or draw on the walls. These behaviours are common and they may not be misbehaviour. Children might be wanting to explore how something feels, like the sound of tearing or the action of knocking down towers. One child I worked with liked to dismantle pop-up books because he wanted to know how they worked. The problem was once they were dismantled, they could no longer pop-up! Our response needs to depend on the age and stage of development of the child. If they are very young the first thing to do is say to the child, 'Wait' or 'Stop' with a clear gesture then try to work out what they are trying to do; for example, if they want to draw, offer them a crayon and paper and say, 'Draw here'. All adults need to respond in the same way by explaining clearly why we do not like what they are doing and always offering an alternative that we would like them to do that taps into a similar action or type of play. Sometimes allowing natural consequences can make the point; for example, if a child breaks a toy, we can't have that toy at nursery anymore until they help us mend it.

Exclusive play and stereotyping

At a young age, children tend to base their stereotypes on physical appearance like skin colour, gender, size and physical disability and by the age of about 4 or 5 we may observe children choosing not to play with another child in a discriminatory way, for example, 'Girls can't climb trees!' Obviously we need to challenge this and encourage a more inclusive approach, whilst accepting that we are not always friends with everyone and that's fine. It is not OK, however, to be unkind, leave someone out of a game or exclude people because they are different from us. There are some great books that address this, for example Michael Rosen's *This Is Our House* (2007) and *When the Dragons Came* by Lynne Moore and Naomi Kefford (2010).

Transitions

Transitions and change can have a huge impact on children's behaviour. Sometimes it can be the really small things that are really big for them. For example, having to go through a different door into our setting, or moving from freeplay to lunchtime. As Daly et al. (2004, p. 111) state, 'Something adults may consider to be a small or insignificant event can be quite traumatic for children'. We need to try to view the world and our settings through our children's eyes to really understand how they feel and what might affect them most. With all transitions we must keep the child central to our discussions and planning and try to involve the child and family as much as possible.

SUPPORTING TRANSITIONS – A STUDENT TEACHER'S PERSPECTIVE

When I was on teaching practice I supported a child who struggled with tidy up time and transitions as a whole. We found giving him warnings before changes in the routine helped, for example five minutes before tidy up time we took a liquid timer to him so that he could watch it. This seemed to ease his anxiety and helped to make transitions smoother.

Here are some ideas of how to support children with transitions during the day:

- View transition times as part of the day, to be planned for and managed.
- Give a time warning to the children, e.g. 'five minutes until we tidy'.
- Use egg timers, sand timers or liquid timers as visual aids.
- Limit waiting times or times when our children have to sit still and be sedentary.
- Be consistent in our routine and responses.
- Offer incentives (e.g. Zara can choose the story today).
- Use songs, rhymes and chants for different parts of the routine, e.g. This is the way we tidy up, tidy up, tidy up...
- Count down to a transition (not up!).

- Pre-empt which children will find it difficult and offer them additional support.
- Use visual timetables and Now/Next cards.

Transitions are not just within the day in our settings. We also have transitions into our setting or into school. Here are some additional ideas to support these transitions:

- Build relationships with parents/settings/school.
- Consider children's holistic development, in particular their emotional needs.
- Share information (e.g. 'All about me' type forms).
- Make chatterboxes and share special things from home.
- Use transitional objects and comforters if needed.
- Share stories about transitions/photos/pictures.
- Engage in role play and puppets.
- Make changes gradually over time.
- Home visits, settling in sessions, transition meetings.
- Offer high-quality information to families (virtual tours / tours, photos, website, prospectus).
- Communicate with all: children, families and staff – formal and informal opportunities to talk.

If the transition is from one age group to another in the same setting or school we can:

- Build relationships with the next teacher and other adults.
- Provide additional opportunities for spending time together prior to the transition.
- Share information with the next carers.
- Begin a project in the old age group which can be continued in the new age group.
- Continue using their learning journey or mark making journal/books in the new room.
- Create a display in the new room with creations made by the children after visiting, which will help the new room feel welcoming and familiar and their contribution valued.

- Ensure adults liaise about management systems, e.g. stopping class or self-registration, and aim for consistency of approach.
- Keep routine of the new age group as similar to the old as possible (particularly immediately after the transition).

ACTIVITY

Imagine you have been asked to lead a parents' support group about behaviour. What are the key messages you will give? Create a hand-out or leaflet to share with parents which outlines the key strategies your setting adopts when promoting positive behaviour.

Concluding thoughts

There are many strategies that we use to support children when they behave in challenging ways and they are all different tools in our behaviour toolbox. We need to select the appropriate tool for the situation and sometimes we may need several! The key messages are to stay calm and respond mindfully rather than reacting emotionally. In addition we need to remain consistent in our response and turn all incidents into opportunities to learn. This will teach children how to deal with their big emotions and how to behave when they feel that way. The next chapter explores this further as we look at how educators can become co-regulators to help children with self-regulation.

QUESTIONS FOR REFLECTION

How many tools do we regularly use in our toolbox when responding to children's behaviour?

Are there any techniques in this chapter we would like to try or practise?

Which challenging behaviour do we find most difficult to deal with? Why might this be? How can we better understand the child and their needs when they behave in this way?

Further reading

Mainstone-Cotton, S. (2020) *Supporting Young Children through Change and Everyday Transitions: Practical Strategies for Practitioners and Parents*. London: Jessica Kingsley Publishers.

Mathieson, K. (2015) *Understanding Behaviour in the Early Years*. London: MA Education.

References

Acredolo, L. & Goodwyn, S. (2009) *Baby Signs: How to Talk with Your Baby Before Your Baby Can Talk*, 3rd edn. New York: McGraw-Hill Education.

Daly, M., Byers, E. & Taylor, W. (2004) *Early Years Management in Practice*. Oxford: Heinemann.

Lavoie, J., Leduc, K., Arruda, C., Crossman, A. & Talwar, V. (2017) Developmental profiles of children's spontaneous lie-telling behavior. *Cognitive Development*, 41, 33–46.

Moore, L. & Kefford, N. (2010) *When the Dragons Came*. New York: Simon & Schuster Children's UK.

Nagar, P., Williams, S. & Talwar, V. (2019) The influence of an older sibling on preschoolers' lie-telling behavior. *Social Development*, 28(4), 1095–1111.

Rosen, M. (2007) *This Is Our House*. London: Walker Books.

Self-regulation and co-regulation

This chapter will explore self-regulation and reframes the idea of 'managing behaviour' into 'supporting' children. Adults help children to develop self-regulation through becoming a co-regulator. It thinks about executive function and how we can help children to develop their social skills. It also explains that it is meaningless to force children to say 'sorry'; instead we need to role model being sorry, teach children to make friends and find alternatives to saying sorry that are more meaningful to the children.

Introduction

Imagine the scene. You have been invited to a major sporting event with your best friend. The big day finally arrives and your alarm doesn't go off! So, with no time for breakfast, you rush off to the station in a panic and meet your friend only to find that the train has been cancelled. There is a replacement bus service running, so you jump aboard and are soon on your way. Pretty soon you run into major roadworks and you realise you might not get to the venue on time. The bus station is not as close to the venue as the train station was, so you now flag down a taxi and pray for green lights and no traffic… Sadly, it is not meant to be as you hit hold up after hold up before arriving at the venue late, hungry and tired. The organisers on the door say you should have got there earlier and refuse to let you in.

It takes every ounce of self-regulation you have not to scream! You can feel your temperature rising and you turn away before you say something you might regret. At this point your friend, always the practical one, stays calm, reminds you to breathe and calm down then explains to the organisers what has happened. She asks if there is any chance you could be allowed in. They have sympathy for your series of unfortunate events and allow you in, escorting you to your seats.

When we are in a stressful situation or feel our blood pressure rising we are not able to think rationally, as explained in Chapter 2. Sometimes as adults, like our friend, we are able to remain calm in the face of adversity or stress, sometimes we need to walk away and sometimes we lose it and flip our lids! When our friend reminded us to breathe and calm down, she was actually becoming a co-regulator and helping us to regulate our own emotions. This is the role we take on with our children as we scaffold them and support them through their big feelings and role model and coach them about how to respond.

Self-regulation

There is a mistaken assumption that self-regulation is simply about children learning to control their own behaviour. This is an oversimplification and neglects the role of other people, putting too much emphasis on the child and their ability to control themselves or inhibit their behaviour. Actually self-regulation involves children coping with their big emotions, sometimes inhibiting their actions, being able to focus on things and having executive function skills, and often self-regulation involves other people and their response to them as well.

So when children have powerful thoughts and emotions, they need to learn how to manage them in order to regain feelings of calm and they will need help from adults to learn this. This is thinking about children in terms of their emotional resilience. When they face an upset or disappointment, will they fall at the first hurdle or will they persevere? Our role is to support children as they work through these feelings and teach them how to respond in the future.

OVERCOMING FRUSTRATION – A PRESCHOOL MANAGER'S PERSPECTIVE

There is a child at preschool who is at the brink of self-care independence which is amazing, however it has also meant many trials, fails and hard lessons for him. He is incredibly proud of all he can do and demonstrates resilience and stamina, but he is reluctant to ask for help and this can lead to him getting extremely frustrated and lashing out when practising his skills. When he starts shouting, kicking and throwing his socks or shoes, we have to consider his safety and that of others whilst equally not undermining his efforts by belittling the task, or stop his expression since all that would teach him is that it is not OK to feel frustrated. As an educator, my first step is to self-regulate, sort of like putting the oxygen mask on yourself first in case of an emergency on a plane.

I need to look at the bigger picture (What is frustrating him? Does he need help? Does he need to simply express himself and, if so, could I suggest a more positive way of expressing how hard he is finding this?). I also need to consider whether I am able to co-regulate (if I do not have the patience today, there are other practitioners who will swap with me and may achieve co-regulation much faster and more calmly).

On one occasion, once I had assessed the situation and ensured the safety of everyone (in this case moving other children into a different space), I sat with the child and offered him a hug. He usually calms himself very quickly when hugged, but I don't like to assume even in situations of distress. Because he was shouting, I simply opened my arms and held them out to him. It meant he didn't need to physically hear me, he could see the cue and choose to react. He climbed onto my lap and we took a couple of deep breaths before exploring the situation together.

Once he was calm I said, 'I can see that you were getting really frustrated when you were putting your socks on. It did look like a really tricky job and I am so proud of how hard you're trying!'

Because I know him as a proud and independent child, I felt praising his efforts whilst simultaneously acknowledging how hard it is might work. He gave his sock a kick and grumpily replied, 'Yes, it's really hard and I just can't do it'. We looked at the sock together and I commented on the cool pink dinosaur on it. This made him giggle as he corrected me, 'it's purple, not pink!' I replied, 'Oh, you're right, I got it wrong. It's purple. Still very cool though! I wonder where the purple dino usually sits on your foot?' The child considered this and answered, 'He sits right here!' (pointing at his toes). I suggested he put his socks in front of his feet, showing the dinosaur on the top to remind him how the sock needed to sit when he was done. He tried this and, with some effort, he managed to pull both of them on. He gave me a celebratory hug before speeding off to show his friend his 'super cool dinosaur'.

The setting manager who shared this case study with me added that the child managed to calm really quickly because they used methods practised in the setting and tapped into her knowledge of his character and sense of humour, whilst helping him to still feel heard, respected and empowered. She allowed him to express himself and resisted the urge to take over and put his socks on for him which would have undermined his independence and ability. She didn't expect him to talk, explain or even listen until he was calm. Apparently, a few days later, he used the same tactics to support one of his friends and help them to calm down when they were struggling. This is our aim, to empower children to know what to do when they feel overwhelmed with emotion and to independently use these strategies in the future.

Self-regulation also includes children being able to inhibit their impulses or stop themselves doing something. For example, if they really want to play with a toy that their friend is playing with, they will need a certain amount of self-regulation to be able to stop themselves from just taking it from their friend. Or if they are feeling very cross about something, it is self-regulation that enables them to not lash out.

Another facet of self-regulation is when children can maintain focus and attention and have high levels of involvement without being easily distracted. It takes quite a lot of self-regulation to remain focused on a task if it becomes difficult. I have heard it said that children operate at their highest cognitive level when engaging in self-initiated activities and we know that when children are fully engaged with high levels of involvement there is less time for poor behaviour and they are more likely to make progress in learning and development.

There are many ways we can help children to develop self-regulation as this chapter explains, however the main way is for adults to act as co-regulators and scaffold children while they have big emotions. One resource that settings and parents find really useful when supporting children is the *Keep Your Cool Toolbox* app by Mine Conkbayir (2020) (see https://keepyourcool-toolbox.com/). It contains simple and effective strategies such as completing puzzles together, breathing exercises and mindful moments to help children regain feelings of calm, and I highly recommend it. One setting manager I have worked with has written a policy entitled *Promoting Self-Regulation through Co-Regulation and a Loving Pedagogy* which outlines how she uses the toolbox within their setting. Chapter 9 explores this in more detail.

Co-regulation

Co-regulation is about working alongside children, interacting in the moment and coaching children through difficult times. There will be times in their lives when children face difficulty and challenges and part of our role as an educator is to teach them appropriate ways of reacting that are calm and forward thinking, resolving problems rather than escalating the situation. This will help them to learn strategies and what to do independently in the future, so we are upskilling our children in helping them to develop self-regulation.

Before we can begin to co-regulate children's emotions, we need to have built warm, loving, trusting and responsive relationships with them. This is so they will listen to us and feel safe and secure (see Chapter 1). It involves our being attuned to the children and their emotional states, so we can recognise when they are getting upset or angry and coach them through the tricky time. Sometimes we can nip things in the bud and prevent issues from escalating; however, we need to be wary of stepping in too soon and preventing the children from resolving problems themselves and having the opportunity to learn. We cannot and should not remove all feelings of frustration, annoyance and even disappointment at not achieving something for children because that would stop them from learning how to problem solve, think creatively and use their initiative. It is not our job to always stop them from failing... but it is our job to instil those qualities that show them that it's OK to fail, it's OK to get it wrong and this is what we do about it. We try and try again. We get up, brush ourselves down and learn from it. If we are resilient and persevere we usually succeed in the end.

Sometimes we will need to coach children while they feel upset or angry, labelling the emotions and helping them to know first that having the feelings themselves is OK, and second that when we have these feelings, this is what we can do... so that they learn that feeling angry sometimes is quite natural, but we must not hit our friend when we feel angry. Knowing our children emotionally is vitally important, as Chapter 5 stresses.

What we are doing is teaching children strategies to use in the future because we won't always be there every time they have a meltdown or emotion explosion. They will need to learn what is and isn't OK in terms of their reactions. Research has shown that when children have higher levels of self-regulation, they are better able to cope with life and the many challenges that life can bring, and in the shorter term will find it easier to meet the demands that attending school will put on them and may achieve more educationally (Vink et al., 2020).

Coping with the emotional aspects of life is difficult at times and is hard for us to teach to children. However, teach it we must if we are to prepare our children for the future. Ways that we will do this is through role modelling and sometimes direct instruction, as well as through stories, rhymes, role playing, imaginative and small world play. We can set up scenarios where a specific character is feeling a certain way and talk to the children about how they might act and react when they feel that way, explaining the implications or impact each option has on others.

TEACHING ABOUT EMOTIONS – AN INTERNATIONAL SCHOOL EARLY YEARS TEACHER'S PERSPECTIVE

We discuss emotions all the time as a result of most texts we read or videos we watch. Sometimes these are specifically chosen for this purpose. We also use puppets and soft toys to act out specific emotions and ask the children to guess how they are feeling. As many of our children do not have English as their first language, it is really important to use visual cues as well as words to express emotions.

In my book *Calling All Superheroes* (Grimmer, 2019) I refer to a superhero anger chart that we used at home with my daughter when she struggled with anger. It contained a five-point scale which had pictures of superheroes who looked at different levels of anger. It was designed to be read from top to bottom with the child pointing to where they were on the scale and trying to get further down to regain feelings of calm. This is another example of how adults can help co-regulate children's big feelings and support them.

SUPERHERO ANGER SCALE (GRIMMER, 2019)

5. I am out of control and feel like I am going to explode. I want to scream and hit. I need to calm down.
4. I am getting very angry and am starting to lose it! I need to walk away.
3. I feel a little out of control or over excited. I want to run away or jump up and down as fast as I can! I need to do something calmer.
2. I feel a little worried or frustrated. I will try to get through this! I need to be careful not to get overwhelmed.
1. I feel good! I'm completely in control! I'm happy!

Executive function

Sometimes people refer to executive function skills when they think about self-regulation. Executive function is a term which relates to skills like decision making, time management and planning and executing plans. It involves having a good working memory, having mental flexibility and being able to problem solve, organise and prioritise. We can help children to develop these skills by role modelling, promoting positive dispositions to learning like resilience and a 'can do' attitude, thinking out loud and explaining to children what we are thinking, doing and why we are doing it that way. We can praise self-control, create an atmosphere of trust and teach children to have a growth mindset.

The Center on the Developing Child at Harvard University (2021) explains that although we begin to develop executive functioning skills before our first birthday, they are not fully developed until we are adults. So it is no wonder that children find this difficult. They suggest that all children have the potential to develop these skills but they are not innate, that is we are not born with them. They rely upon adults supporting and teaching children in a manner that develops these skills and scaffolds their learning.

One aspect that is particularly tricky is mental flexibility, which is when children are able to cope with changing plans or last-minute changes to their routine, as well as being able to shift their thinking quickly from one task to another. We can help children with this by adding a change or surprise card to our visual timetables which we use when there has been a change. We can also explain to children what has happened and why we need to change our plans. If possible, we can also involve the children in our new plans. The more we can explain and help children to understand the easier the change will be.

Metacognition

Many early childhood educators invite children to plan or revisit their learning, perhaps by using floor books. They might find out what children already know and can do in relation to a specific subject and then plan enhancements to their continuous provision that will expand their knowledge and grow their skills. Then reflecting upon learning with children afterwards is an important element of this process because it encourages children to use their working memory, to think about things they have done and return to our previous learning and thinking – we sometimes call this metacognition, and it is an important skill for children to learn.

REFLECTING ON LEARNING – A NURSERY TEACHER'S PERSPECTIVE

Children love to look at pictures of themselves and talk about work they have done. I have found that a floor book is an ideal stage from which to showcase their work and is more easily accessible than a high display board. Looking back through a floor book with a child is also a really good tool to encourage thinking and reflecting on our learning together. But looking at a big book or floor book is more than just an academic exercise. It is about building a sense of pride in what we have done together, demonstrating to the children that their work is valued and giving the child an opportunity to find their voice.

Metacognition gives us insights into our thoughts, feelings and behaviour and helps us to understand why we have done things a certain way. By encouraging children to reflect on their thinking in this way it helps them to become more resilient as a learner. Although separate from executive function, it is linked. If we find it difficult or frustrating to complete a task this may be due to our developing executive function skills, however if we think about why we find it frustrating or reflect upon the difficult aspects of the task, we might be able to overcome them. This is using metacognition to help solve the problem.

Questions we can ask or talk through with the children before, during and after activities that encourage metacognition are in the table below:

Before	During	After
• What do I already know about this?	• What might happen?	• What have I learned?
• What do I want to find out about or do?	• Am I following my plan?	• Did I meet my goal?
• How can I do this?	• Do I need to try a different method?	• What worked well?
• What am I trying to achieve?	• Can I make links to other times I have tried something similar?	• What might I change next time?
• What resources or materials might I need?	• How will I know if I have been successful?	• Did I enjoy doing or completing this?
• Can anyone help me?	• What am I learning?	• What was my favourite part?

Social interaction

Children are learning in a social context in our settings and learning how to build relationships with others. So the development of self-regulation is also linked with social interaction and children's social development. Understanding concepts like sharing, and the fact that some things belong to other people so we can't always have what we want when we want it, is difficult. These things also rely upon children having some Theory of Mind and, as discussed in Chapter 3, this is not usually developed until 4 or 5 years old.

We need to help children to develop friendships and learn how to relate to others socially. Here are a few ideas of how we can develop children's social skills whilst also building their self-regulation:

- Encourage children to learn and use each other's names.
- Play games together such as parachute games, traffic lights (starting and stopping) games, musical bumps and statues.
- Encourage children to turn-take and share resources and play games involving collaboration.
- Plan group times when children share aspects about their lives to get to know each other better.
- Provide opportunities for joint projects like large-scale construction where children will need to work together to succeed.
- Create cosy spaces where children can sit and chat in small groups.
- Offer open-ended resources that lend themselves to den building.
- Provide books, puppets and resources that help children explore friendship.
- Ensure that our role play areas include resources and materials that reflect children's lives and communities.
- Display photographs of our children's families and other special people and encourage the children to share about their lived experiences with their friends.

As this list shows, our learning environment can also promote children's self-regulation skills. We need to consider the resources we share, the layout of our room and our routine. Can we provide a stimulating and challenging learning environment which also offers opportunities for calm and peaceful times? Is our environment both physically and emotionally safe offering predictable and consistent routines?

Managing behaviour or supporting behaviour?

Behaviour courses and policies used to be framed around managing children's behaviour. I have a problem with this, because this brings in a power dynamic again. It sees the child as an inferior person who needs to be bossed about and managed, rather than a competent person who needs support to manage their own behaviour and emotions. The 'managing' bit needs to be what we are teaching the child to do, rather than us managing the child in the first place.

So instead of looking at managing children's behaviour, we can look at supporting their behaviour or promoting positive behaviour. This changes the focus and removes the idea of us being in charge. We need to be alongside children in this journey of discovery to scaffold and support them and teach them strategies they can use in the future when we're not there. We are co-constructing knowledge and skills together. Chapter 9 thinks about how we can embed these ideas into policy.

Saying sorry and more meaningful alternatives

I have regularly heard parents and carers literally forcing their child to apologise to another child after an incident. As a parent I understand the pressure of wanting your child to conform and to be liked by the other children (and parents). However, we need to think about whether making children say sorry to each other is developmentally appropriate in the early years. Let's think about what being sorry means.

Sorry is partly a social convention, which is employed to help smooth things over after an incident, so it's a phrase learned which can help with, to use an Americanism, closure. But sorry is more than that. If someone is truly sorry, they are actually saying I will try not to do that again. When someone is sorry they are feeling regret or apologetic for causing someone else to be unhappy. Sorry is about repentance and that stems from the idea of turning around and a complete change of direction. Doing a 180… I was doing this, now I'm doing the opposite… So if we are truly sorry, we will actively try not to behave in that way again.

This is a difficult concept for young children to understand. In order to fully comprehend they need to have developed some empathy and have Theory of Mind, which, as Chapter 3 explains, they will not have fully developed within early childhood. So we need to talk to children about being sorry and try to explain what it means in terms of our future actions. Using a mantra like, 'Sorry means you won't do it again' can help. We can role model saying sorry to others, but avoid forcing children to say sorry. It is just a word, however it is a word which other people sometimes place a lot of importance on, so we must explain to our children that sometimes saying sorry to someone else can help them know that we didn't mean to hurt them and we will try not to do it again. We can encourage children to demonstrate they are sorry in more developmentally appropriate ways, for example by giving the other child the toy, by giving them a hug or cuddle, or by playing with them later in the day. These alternatives are more meaningful because they actively demonstrate our remorse and regret in a tangible way.

We do need to ensure we use the word sorry around children and role model how to apologise for a mistake or hurtful action or comment. In the same way that we might role model saying please and thank you, we can role model saying sorry. Sometimes you may want to set up a scenario where you take something from a colleague in front of the children and then demonstrate how to say sorry and act sorry afterwards, talking it through with the children. We can also do this using puppets or soft toys who may need to demonstrate they are sorry to someone else.

SAYING SORRY – A PRESCHOOL'S PERSPECTIVE

We never ask a child to say sorry, it's just a word. We will some-times use phrases like, 'I wonder what we could do to make XXX feel better…?' which allows the child to think about the situation and perhaps offer their thoughts about what they can do to make things better. This means that their learning experience is more pronounced than just being told what to do or say by an adult. All these small incidences give children the experience of positive reinforcement, even when their behaviours have initially been negative. Having a culture of positivity and support, whatever the behaviour, rather than punishment and shame, means that children will, over time, be able to suggest their own solutions to problems or issues they may have. To be able to recognise when they feel angry/frustrated/sad etc. and actually voice that more readily. Which, in turn, will reduce nega-tive behaviour or 'acting out' to get attention. The attention is readily there, without the need to try to get it in a different way.

Finding waiting difficult

Many children find waiting difficult and this is also linked to self-regulation. Even waiting for something we really want is hard. There was a famous test which looked at delaying gratification called the marshmallow test which has been repeated recently by Watts et al. (2018). The original research found a link between children who can delay gratification (wait for more marshmallows) and higher academic achievement later in life. Interestingly, the new replicated research suggests that once we take other factors into account, such as socio-economic status, home environment or gender and ethnicity, the correlation is much weaker and perhaps not statistically significant. However, the new study does demonstrate that home life and intelligence will determine later achievement (Watts et al., 2018). Regardless of whether waiting and having patience helps children's future success, waiting can cause us problems in our settings.

If possible, remove waiting times or significantly reduce them. There is no need to set ourselves and the children up to fail by having times in our routine when children are expected to wait. We are causing ourselves problems which could easily be avoided. If we only have three sinks for washing hands, send children in threes to the toilets to wash hands and keep the rest of the group busy. Singing songs and rhymes are a great way of doing this. One adult or child can lead a song, while another adult ushers children to wash hands.

Schools can be notorious for this – some classes are expected to wait for a runner to tell them when assembly is starting or when dinner is ready... If we need to wait for this, keep the children entertained. Have a box of fidgets available or give every child a poppet and practice your number bonds... If we need to line the children up for any reason, this is the perfect opportunity to practice marching, action songs or balancing on one leg! Better still change the routine to avoid waiting times altogether!

ZARA'S BEAN – A NURSERY TEACHER'S PERSPECTIVE

I planned a bean planting activity based on a conversation I had with a couple of children during lunch at nursery and set up a provocation to allow the children to plant their own beans. It was hugely beneficial to the children's learning and resulted in all children taking their beans home a month later to care for with the help of their parents. All the children were engaged in the activity, however I had one child, Zara, who was so excited about her particular bean that all she wanted was to hold her bean in its pot. This distracted the children and took my attention away from the activity with the others. I had planned for the children to order their beans and for us to measure them, discussing whose bean had grown the tallest. Everyone else was on task and enjoyed using the ruler to measure their beans. At the time, I didn't want Zara to lose out on the teaching moment as I saw it, however she found waiting really difficult and it took lots of my time and energy to keep her involved. On reflection I realised I should just have given Zara her bean and continued the activity with the other children. In that moment, in Zara's world, the only thing that mattered was her bean and she may well have joined the activity again after she had held her bean for a little while. Zara was also the youngest child in our group and the older children were able to understand that they will all be taking their bean home after our activity. This was a very important learning moment for me and only happened because I reflected on the situation afterwards and how I could have better supported Zara and removed the demand for her to wait. Next time, I will think about waiting times and truly listen to the children.

 **ACTIVITY**

Ask a colleague or family member to play this game with you. It is called, 'Oh no! But…' Your partner will start by saying something disastrous starting with the phrase, 'Oh no!' For example, 'Oh no, our house is on fire!' Then you are going to cancel everything your partner says to you by saying the opposite or a reason why this really isn't a problem, starting with the word, 'But…' For example, 'But it's OK because the fire brigade put the fire out…' Then the game continues… 'Oh no, the smoke is making me cough…' 'But I've opened a window so the smoke has cleared…'

See how many times you can respond and act as a co-regulator for your partner by calming the situation down.

Concluding thoughts

Self-regulation is sometimes misunderstood and simplified to self-control. Although this is part of the story, this chapter has explained that self-regulation is much broader than this, including elements like executive function, focus and attention, social interaction and much more. The role of the adult is vital in supporting children's self-regulation and the main way that they support their children is through co-regulation. In addition, educators can use their knowledge of repetitive play, sometimes referred to as schemas, to redirect children's behaviour, as the next chapter explores.

QUESTIONS FOR REFLECTION

How can we become co-regulators for our children?
What does a learning environment which promotes self-regulation look like in practice?
What is our first step in developing or further developing children's self-regulation in our setting?

Further reading

Center on the Developing Child, Harvard University (2021) *Executive Function & Self-Regulation*. Retrieved from https://developingchild .harvard.edu/science/key-concepts/executive-function/

Conkbayir, M. (2020) *Keep Your Cool Toolbox*. Retrieval from https:// keepyourcooltoolbox.com/

Grimmer, T. & Geens, W. (2022) *Nurturing Self-regulation in Early Childhood: Adopting an Ethos and Approach*. London: Routledge.

References

Center on the Developing Child, Harvard University (2021) *Executive Function & Self-Regulation.* Available at https://developingchild.harvard.edu/science/key-concepts/executive-function/

Conkbayir, M. (2020) *Keep Your Cool Toolbox.* Available at https://keepyourcooltoolbox.com/

Grimmer, T. (2019) *Calling All Superheroes: Supporting and Developing Superhero Play in the Early Years.* London: Routledge.

Vink, M., Gladwin, T.E., Geeraerts, S., Pas, P., Bos, D., Hofstee, M., Durston, S. & Vollebergh, W. (2020) Towards an integrated account of the development of self-regulation from a neurocognitive perspective: A framework for current and future longitudinal multimodal investigations. *Developmental Cognitive Neuroscience,* 45. doi: 10.1016/j.dcn.2020.100829

Watts, T., Duncan, G. & Quan, H. (2018) Revisiting the marshmallow test: A conceptual replication investigating links between early delay of gratification and later outcomes, *Psychological Science,* 29(7), 1159–1177.

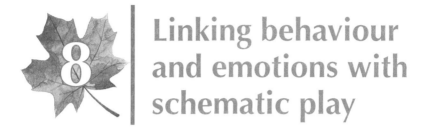

Linking behaviour and emotions with schematic play

Sometimes children behave in confusing or intriguing ways that are difficult for us to fathom, for example always throwing things, plugging the sink with tissue paper, or unravelling the toilet roll. These behaviours can be described as schematic, when children engage in repetitive behaviours or actions. This chapter reinterprets these behaviours as schematic and considers how we can respond more appropriately by finding the children an alternative experience which taps into their fascination or schema.

Introduction

When I became a parent I had the luxury and opportunity to observe very young children on a daily basis. My daughters all played in schematic ways and as an educator I found it interesting to note this behaviour. I actually turned into a schema evangelist, someone who wanted to spread the word about this type of play at every given opportunity. At the toddler group, when a parent would sigh and say how frustrated they were with their toddler throwing food, I would pipe up, 'Don't worry it's not naughtiness, it's just a schema and really common in this age…' Or at the park when a carer might say, 'My son just wants to be pushed on the swing continually… I wonder why!' I would reply, 'It's a schema – he loves the back and forth trajectory movement!' I'm sure I must have unintentionally annoyed a few friends along the way!

On a serious note, upon reflection, I feel that having this understanding made me a better parent, because I was able to reinterpret their actions and accept it as play more readily. I wish I had known

DOI: 10.4324/9781003137474-9

about schemas when I was a newly qualified teacher. I can still remember when two lads in my class blocked the sinks with green paper towels, much to the horror of our caretaker. I didn't know why they did it at the time, but I did think it was quite scientific. They would proudly ask me to come and see the water that was overflowing and then wonder why I calmly asked them to stop and unclog the sink… I wish I had been able to recognise this as schematic play and given them an alternative place to play which would tap into the same curiosity. Hindsight is a wonderful thing, and I know that with additional knowledge and understanding about schemas educators will be more effective in supporting children's behaviour and emotions.

What are schemas?

When children engage in repetitive behaviours or actions, this can be described as schematic. For example, we might see children lining up toy animals, spinning the wheels of toy cars or continually filling and emptying resource boxes. In my book *Observing and Developing Schematic Behaviour in Young Children* (Grimmer, 2017), I identify 12 common schemas and unpick what they might look like in practice. I explore several case studies and the children's possible lines of enquiry and how adults can support and extend their play.

Schemas help children to represent and develop their ideas about the world through repeated actions or thinking. Everyone's brains learn through repetition so playing in schematic ways strengthens our brain and is a natural way to explore and investigate. If we think about this in terms of children, when a child brings us the same book… again… even if we've already read it five times today, we still need to read the book, because their brain needs the repetition of this story. Hearing the language in the book again is helping them to learn and building their brain.

Common schemas

The table shows a list of the common schemas I wrote about in my book (Grimmer, 2017) and explains what we might see in practice.

Schema	What we might see children doing
Connection	Children joining and connecting materials or objects together, e.g. connecting the train track, trucks or using any type of tape, string or bands to connect materials.
Containing	Children filling and emptying lots of containers and/or bags repeatedly, e.g. placing items in the bin, filling handbags or boxes. This can also include children containing themselves as they play inside boxes, and links with enclosing and enveloping.
Core and radial	Children who enjoy combining trajectory and rotation schemas, e.g. drawing suns (lines coming out from a core) or building constructions or creations with lines coming out from a central point.
Enclosing	Children enclosing themselves in spaces, climbing into boxes, tunnels or pop up houses. They may also draw borders around their mark making or construct enclosures around themselves or small world animals with bricks or other equipment. Links with containing and enveloping.
Enveloping	Children who like to hide or be covered up, e.g. they may dress up in layers of clothing including hats. They might enjoy wrapping up dolls and teddy bears in blankets and/or play peek-a-boo or 'hide and seek'. Links with enclosing and containing.
Going through a boundary	Children who have a fascination with doors, windows or moving things into and out of spaces, e.g. shape sorters, posting, going through tunnels and doors. Can include opening and closing.
Orientation	Children who try to see things from different angles, e.g. looking through their legs, lying on their backs with legs up or upside down on a sofa etc. Wanting to always be under or on top of things. Peeping through holes or looking at the world through binoculars or magnifying glasses.
Positioning	Children interested in where things are, e.g. lining up toys, arranging things by size, walking around sand tray edges or preferring food not to touch other foods, or always wanting a particular colour. It can also include children lying on floors or under tables.
Rotation	Children interested in anything that spins or rolls, e.g. watching the washing machine or rolling down hills, spinning themselves, riding on roundabouts or preferring round objects. Some children may be fascinated with balls or wheeled toys including bicycle wheels.
Trajectory	Children who throw or use their body in a trajectory action, e.g. dropping items of food from cots, high chairs etc. Playing with running water from taps, building and knocking down towers, climbing on and jumping off furniture, bouncing or kicking balls.

(Continued)

Schema	What we might see children doing
Transforming	Children who explore and like to see changes, e.g. adding colour to cornflour, mixing paints together, making or manipulating play dough, adding juice to food, adding water to sand and mixing potions.
Transporting	Children moving objects from one area to another, sometimes with their hands, in bags or via doll's prams or trolleys. They may like to push their friends around in pushchairs or transport sand/water from one area to another.

Supporting and extending schemas

Schemas are not random, they tend to be methodical, logical and systematic ways of learning where children are gathering information through their senses, and interacting with people, objects and the environment. If we identify schemas in our children's play we can then use this to plan their next steps by building on their fascinations and interests. When we plan specific opportunities for children which follow up on their schemas it is as if we are presenting them with a gift or an opportunity to use the materials. If they want to, they may naturally extend their schematic play using the resources or materials that we have provided. This is another way of enhancing our continuous provision, which we offer every day.

When we tune into children and observe them playing in repetitive ways, we can use our knowledge of this to support them emotionally and physically by:

- Offering genuine interest in what they are doing.
- Asking ourselves what are the children interested in or fascinated by.
- Supporting and challenging their thinking and play.
- Providing resources that the child may need or we feel will support this schema.
- Setting up appropriate provocations to support this schema.
- Adjusting the learning environment to include more opportunities for this play.
- Reviewing our relationships in terms of positive interaction.
- Sharing what we have observed with parents/carers.

Reinterpreting behaviour

Children do many puzzling things and will often repeat these behaviours. It is highly likely that they may be misinterpreted as challenging when they could simply be schematic. Therefore having an understanding of schematic play helps us to think about children's behaviour. Some examples of schematic play that can be misinterpreted include:

- Throwing toys or resources.
- Kicking or hitting.
- Jumping on or off or climbing on furniture.
- Unravelling a toilet roll or pulling all the tissues from a tissue box.
- Emptying containers out onto the floor.
- Opening and shutting or playing with doors and windows.
- Smearing food all over themselves or the table.
- Pouring their drink onto their food.
- Knocking down towers.
- Taking toys apart or dismantling things.
- Playing with running water.
- Plugging sinks.
- Posting resources down the back of radiators.
- Mixing sand and water.
- Putting toys in their pockets.
- Collecting toys and resources and moving them around.
- Not wanting foods to touch each other.
- Only wanting a certain coloured plate/bowl/cup/toy.

Before I knew about schemas I would have suggested that a child who was jumping and throwing things needed to stop jumping and throwing and I would probably have offered them alternative activities that didn't involve jumping or throwing. As these alternatives were not trajectory it was unlikely that the child would be interested in them and they probably continued jumping and throwing despite my attempts to stop them! Instead I needed to offer the child trajectory play that was acceptable in the circumstances, e.g. splatter painting, home-made throwing games, the marble run, water play with pipes and gutters etc. The child would be more likely to be interested in this trajectory play and it might redirect them away from the activities that were more disruptive.

If we can better understand children's schemas we can accept behavioural differences and schematic behaviour and use our knowledge of the children's interests and fascinations to provide appropriate alternatives to unacceptable behaviour. As Nutbrown states, 'Many professional educators use what they know about schemas to divert children from disruptive activities and to focus them on more worthwhile endeavours' (Nutbrown, 2011, p. 22).

So we're being schematic behaviour detectives and trying to decide what the child is thinking about or investigating or feeling. We need to delve deeper and consider it in more detail. You could think of it as possible lines of enquiry. Schemas provide a new lens with which to view these children and in doing so redirect them and better support their play.

JAYDON'S TOWERS – A PRESCHOOL'S PERSPECTIVE

Jaydon is a busy 2 ½ year old who loves playing in the construction area and builds continually at every opportunity. When other children are playing near him, he enjoys knocking down their towers, which often ends up with the other children being upset. We try to talk to him about how the other children feel when he has knocked down their towers but it doesn't stop him. We recognise this as a schema, so we have tried to encourage Jaydon to build in his own space and sometimes played alongside him, allowing him to knock down our towers. We are working on getting him to ask before knocking down. We have given the children carpet squares to build on to try to help Jaydon to stay in his space.

It would be easy to be concerned if we had a child like Jaydon who keeps knocking towers down and playing in a destructive way, however he could be investigating disconnecting which links with the connection schema, and also enjoying the trajectory movement involved with knocking down the towers. If we stop to think about it, children receive mixed messages from us as adults. One of the first games we play with children when they start to show an interest in block play is encouraging them to knock the tower down. We build it, they knock it down, we clap. Then at some point we expect them to stop knocking them down and to build instead, but I don't think this is ever communicated to the children!

By viewing children's play as schematic we remove any element of judgement and we will try to find alternatives for them, just as the preschool educators have played alongside Jaydon building towers specifically for him to knock down. We could also involve children in stacking games such as Jenga. We could redirect their attention into activities involving trajectory movement or connecting and disconnecting which might capture their attention. We can also work alongside them to help them understand how the action of knocking down a tower impacts on the other children. Using schemas to reinterpret children's challenging behaviour gives us, as educators, another tool for our toolbox.

ON/OFF – A NURSERY EDUCATOR'S PERSPECTIVE

Caleb kept running over to the door and jumping up and down as if he wanted to go out of the room. As a nursery we offer loose parts play and were particularly interested when Caleb began to build using large wooden blocks and crates next to the door. We realised he was trying to reach the light switch. He successfully built high enough for him to reach and then repeatedly turned the switch on and off saying, 'Off… On…' as he did so. Caleb did this again and again over several days. We decided to create a switch board for him, which consisted of different types of switches screwed to a board which we left out for him to access. It was a great success and he loved it!

It would have been easy for the nursery educators to stop Caleb from climbing and also switching the lights on and off, however they recognised this as schematic and came up with the ingenious idea of the switch board. This meant they could redirect his play with the light switches elsewhere.

127

Schemas and emotions

Sometimes schemas are linked with emotions too. In her book which explores schemas and emotions, Arnold talks about her grandson, Harry, who was really into connecting everything with string (Arnold & The Penn Green Team, 2010). She had studied his interest in connection, without looking at it through an emotional lens initially, then when she later reflected upon this phase in his life, she noticed that there was a link between his strong desire to connect and his emotional world. Harry's parents had separated and he was trying to connect everything else together! Arnold realised that there was often an emotional significance to schematic play and she states, 'Cognition in action can assist young children in processing and coming to understand very real emotional events in their lives' (Arnold & The Penn Green Team, 2010, p. 3).

LYRA'S INTEREST IN DRESSING UP – A PRESCHOOL'S PERSPECTIVE

Lyra attended our setting every day and on arrival she would always go to the same space and resource – she absolutely loved dressing up and without fail, arrived in the busy preschool and headed for the rail of dressing up clothes. As educators we were concerned that Lyra had narrow interests and wondered what would happen if we didn't set out the dressing up straight away. We hoped that this would encourage Lyra to engage with something else… But we had underestimated the emotional support that this repeated action was giving her. On this occasion Lyra was devastated – she was really distraught and could not settle in at all – in fact, we had to get the dressing up out anyway! Lyra was using her repetitive behaviour to help her to feel safe, secure and comfortable in the setting. When this was taken away, the rug was literally pulled from under her and her emotional support was removed. We have made sure we have the dressing up available for Lyra every day since.

This emotional significance was true for Lyra as well as Harry. She was using the repetition of familiar play to support herself emotionally, and as a transitional object, enabling her to confidently join in with setting life. Whilst being detectives we can also be on the lookout for emotional links from their play, using schemas as an additional lens. I have noticed this in my own children's play, with my youngest engaging in several lines of enquiry involving rope, tying knots and connecting things when we moved house. On reflection, I wonder if tying things together as her world changed around her was her way of coping with the move.

As mentioned before, we are never certain why a child behaves in a specific way and we cannot state with certainty that they play in this way because… full stop. We are making educated guesses and creating a working hypothesis which helps us to interpret what we see, hear and observe. We are then trying to use these ideas to better support the child.

Schemas and additional needs

Schemas are not, in themselves, an indication of additional needs. All children, regardless of their level of need, both neurotypical and neurodiverse, could play in schematic ways. I am often asked about schemas in relation to autism spectrum disorder or condition (ASD/ASC). This is a neurological condition so people with autism experience the world differently and their brain functions in a slightly different way to neurotypical people, that is people who do not have ASC.

I am choosing to use 'condition' rather than 'disorder' because using the word disorder is a deficit model and implies something is wrong therefore it is a negative way of viewing autism, whereas it is actually about difference. As a parent of children with ASC, I have noticed that the language we use is important.

Many young children engage in repetitive behaviours at some point, however we may see more repetitive play from children with ASC. In fact, repetitive, ritualised and compulsive behaviours form part of the diagnosis, however they are a very small part of a much bigger picture. Therefore, I want to be clear that schematic play is not an indication of ASC or any other additional needs. Diagnosis also focuses on social interaction, social communication and their use of imagination. If we had any concerns about a child, we would want to build as big a picture as possible and not simply worry about a child lining up toys for example. Repetitive behaviours and obsessions are by no means the whole picture.

We may ask ourselves additional questions to focus our observations if we are concerned about a child, for example:

- Can the child communicate with us?
- Do they respond to their own name?
- Do they appear to not hear some of the time, but hear fine at others?
- Do they make eye contact?
- Do they point?
- Can they share attention with us?
- Do they show an interest in other children?
- Will they naturally smile back at us when we smile at them?

Sometimes our role is to reassure parents and carers who may notice their children playing schematically and not realise that this is typical play for a young child. Many settings offer schema workshops for parents and carers and share information about schemas with them. Feel free to share the chart from earlier in this chapter showing schemas and what we might see children doing for each schema. It might help explain these behaviours to parents and carers.

Another thing I want to mention in relation to schemas is children who always want, for example, the green cup and the green plate or green toys, and woe betide anyone who tries to give them a different colour! I personally feel this behaviour is probably schematic and another example of mis-diagnosing it as poor behaviour. Schemas are really strong urges sometimes and so if a child has a strong green schema, they will want everything to be green at the moment. And perhaps our first response should be, 'Why not?' Sometimes adults think about children in terms of us versus them, for example, we mustn't let them get their own way all the time... but for the child, it's not a war but it is a really strong feeling that life is OK when I have a green plate and it's not OK when I don't. In fact, it really is the end of the world when I don't have one. As adults, who see the bigger picture, we might see this as insignificant, it's only a plate after all, but for that child, at that moment, it means such a lot. They don't have bills to pay, or a fast spreading virus to worry about, they act and react in the moment. If we can do something simple like hand out a plate that helps a child to feel happy, safe and secure, why would we choose to deliberately do something that makes them unhappy?

I have shared this idea with educators in the past and some have answered along the lines of, 'That's all very well, Tamsin, but we only have one green plate and if we always let Georgia have it, then it's not fair on the others...' I do take this point, but would ask if the other children care about the colour as much as Georgia, and if it really is coveted, then why on earth do we only have one! It would be very easy to get another couple of green plates! When we're handing the plates out, we have a choice, we can hand them out randomly and tell the children they can't choose their colour, which may end in tears for Georgia, or we can use a bit of sleight of hand and make sure that Georgia gets the green plate and thus avoid a tantrum and make our lives easier! We don't need to make a big thing of it, we just do it quietly and no one will notice, except perhaps Georgia. It's not pandering to her, it's being wise and avoiding an incident. On reflection, we may find we do this already; for example, we know the child who does not want a broken breadstick and when we're handing them out we try to find a whole one for that child.

This links with my work around developing a loving pedagogy (Grimmer, 2021) and tapping into children's love languages (Chapman and Campbell, 2012). We have the ability to do something kind and loving that will help a child feel thought about and loved. Holding children in mind and doing things specifically for them is part of this, even if it is giving them a green plate!

ACTIVITY

This letter was written to an Agony Aunt about behaviour (which is schematic). Imagine you are Sympathetic Sue – how would you respond?

Dear Sympathetic Sue,
My son is driving me crazy! Johnnie is 18 months old now and keeps dropping his beaker from his high chair, again and again! As soon as he drops it, he looks at me to pick it up for him. When I

do and place it on his tray, he immediately drops it again! He will repeat this until I get fed up and stop giving it back to him. Please help!

From Frustrated in Ferryport

Concluding thoughts

It would be very easy to attribute children's puzzling and repetitive behaviour as them misbehaving or seeing it as something we should try to stop. However, it is my view that many of these actions are schematic with children following their own lines of enquiry. Viewing it in this way gives our observation a more positive slant and enables us to better understand the child, since all behaviour, schematic play included, is communication. Then we can think creatively about how to embrace these schemas through the environment we provide, the ethos we foster and the way we accept their play. The next chapter thinks a little more about our ethos and also how we can work in partnerships with others when supporting children's behaviour and emotions.

QUESTIONS FOR REFLECTION

Have we observed any schemas in our children's play?
Can we reinterpret any observed behaviour in the light of schemas?
How can we share about schemas with parents and carers?

Further reading

Arnold, C. & The Penn Green Team (2010) *Understanding Schemas and Emotion in Early Childhood*. London: Sage.

Grimmer, T. (2017) *Observing and Developing Schematic Behaviour in Young Children: A Professional Guide for Supporting Children's Learning, Play and Development*. London: Jessica Kingsley Publishers.

Louis, S. (2013) *Schemas and the Characteristics of Effective Learning*. London: Early Education.

References

Arnold, C. & The Penn Green Team (2010) *Understanding Schemas and Emotion in Early Childhood*. London: Sage.

Chapman, G. & Campbell, R. (2012) *The 5 Love Languages of Children*. Chicago, IL: Northfield Publishing.

Grimmer, T. (2017) *Observing and Developing Schematic Behaviour in Young Children: A Professional Guide for Supporting Children's Learning, Play and Development*. London: Jessica Kingsley Publishers.

Grimmer, T. (2021) *Developing a Loving Pedagogy in the Early Years: How Love Fits with Professional Practice*. London: Routledge.

Nutbrown, C. (2011) *Threads of Thinking*, 4th edn. London: Sage.

9 Our ethos and partnerships

This chapter will think about how our policy and practice should be underpinned by our ethos when working with young children. It will share the idea of developing a loving pedagogy and how this can provide a foundation for our practice and explain why I feel we need to avoid reward charts. It will consider the important role that parents and carers play as the child's first educator and the importance and benefits of collaboration. It will also think about the other professionals that practitioners may need to liaise with in order to better support the child.

Introduction

It is vitally important that what we believe in and our ethos underpin our practice. When considering policy and practice, we need to begin with our approach and ethos. This should then have a direct impact on our practice, because what we believe should influence how we act and respond to the children. So our practice should match our ethos. We then write our policies with our ethos and practice in mind, rubber stamping what we do and why we do it. So all three should align together – with our approach and ethos as the foundation on which everything else is built. For me, I believe we need to adopt a loving pedagogy so that love is part of this foundation.

DOI: 10.4324/9781003137474-10

Loving pedagogy

It might sound odd talking in terms of love in relation to early childhood practice. Despite the caring nature of our role, love and loving are words that are not readily used in our settings. I have recently explored this in my book, *Developing a Loving Pedagogy in the Early Years* (Grimmer, 2021), and I believe that we do love the children in our care and should not shy away from using this terminology. If we are truly seeking to understand our children and their behaviour we would be better placed to do this if we have an emotional connection with them, and it would be impossible to separate this from love.

What do I mean by a loving pedagogy? Well it might be easier to explain if we unpick and consider how a parent loves their child. The love they have for their child is more than a feeling, it also involves action. They look after them and keep them safe, always with their best interests at heart, they plan activities with their child in mind and think about them when they are not together. They do things for them, like cooking their favourite meals, and regularly tell them they love them. Most educators I know feel and act in this way with regard to the children in their care; wanting the best for the children, holding them in mind and putting their needs first. We tend to talk about pedagogy within education to mean everything we are doing to lead and teach our children. From the approach we adopt and ethos we foster to the strategies we employ by tapping into children's fascinations and interests, and taking into consideration their needs, backgrounds and strengths as we plan the learning environment and interact with them. By using the phrase 'a loving pedagogy' I aim to combine the caring aspects of our role with our practice and describe an approach to working with children that can underpin all aspects of our provision.

Avoid reward-based systems

Whilst considering our ethos and approach we need to think about our response to rewards-based systems. Many advice books adopt a behavioural approach which focuses on positive reinforcement of behaviours we want to repeat and sanctions or punishment when children behave in ways we do not want to see again. For example, they may suggest using reward charts, having sunshine/cloud or traffic light systems to help promote positive behaviour. Usually a child will have their picture or name moved from one place to another depending on how they behave. There are many problems with this approach. These systems are based on 'extrinsic motivation', that is, we are rewarded when we behave and punished when we don't, rather than 'intrinsic motivation' which is when we do something because we want to or find it rewarding in itself. They also have an unequal power dynamic so children must obey the adults and do what they say simply because the adult has said so and they shame children into obedience.

Reward-based systems often work because many children want to please adults and are frightened of making mistakes and upsetting their carers. They do not want to be 'told off'. Fear of being 'put on the cloud' or 'given a red card' is at the heart of these methods. However, systems based on fear should have no place in our early childhood settings and schools and do not fit within a loving, child-centred pedagogy. After all, as Jung and Smith (2018) point out, as educators compliance is not our long-term goal. We actually want children to become good learners, to adopt positive dispositions to learning and grow in confidence. We are aiming for children to have success as a life-long learner and grow to make a positive contribution to society and meet their own potential. I really love this quote from Lungu (2018, p. 235) which challenges us to think about why we are using reward-based systems: 'Do we want to form some obedient, humble, subservient person, dependent on the approval and appreciation of others or do we want autonomous, independent, responsible people with a good image and positive self-esteem?' If compliance and dependence is our aim, perhaps we should change careers!

The vast majority of children who experience these systems will stay on the positive sunshine, rainbow or green card most of the time; however, there will be a small minority of children for whom these systems add to their low self-esteem and unbelief in themselves. They will wonder what is the point of conforming when their names are seldom removed from the 'unwanted behaviour' sections. Using this approach is counter to a trauma informed, attachment aware approach and can lead to our most vulnerable children feeling misunderstood and unsupported, and it can also trigger stress and anxiety.

Publicly shaming or disciplining a child in front of others is unhelpful and should be avoided. Children tend to react badly to this, with many deliberately continuing with the unwanted behaviour because they are on show. Instead, move closer to the child, get down to their level and ask them to stop. Use a clear 'No' or 'Stop' hand signal or sign and maintain gentle body language and ensure our tone of voice does not sound aggressive. We can be clear and firm without sounding angry or too harsh. Keeping calm ourselves is vital, and if we are unable to remain calm we need to remove ourselves from the situation.

Our approach to behaviour needs to be non-judgemental and focused on understanding why children are behaving the way they are. Again, we are back to the idea of all behaviour being communication, focusing on acknowledging feelings and supporting children emotionally. We need to listen to children, reflect upon their behaviour and become the behaviour detectives mentioned in Chapter 5. When we adopt this approach there is no sliding scale of poor behaviour, with no winners and losers; instead there are children who are experiencing big feelings and have not yet learned how to cope with them and are being supported by the adults caring for them.

REWARD CHARTS – A CHILDMINDER'S PERSPECTIVE

I'm not keen on the concepts of gaining/losing rewards or children being on colour-coded warnings etc. The evidence I have read about the brain and our neurological pathways suggests this approach is not helpful. However seeing all behaviour as communication is a better approach to adopt because it supports each child.

Parents as the first educators

Parents and carers are children's first educators and know our children very well. We must never underestimate this and working in partnership is vitally important. Many children may behave very differently in our settings when compared with how they behave at home. Some children are so different that their parents could be forgiven for asking the educator if they're talking about the same child! I call these children Jekyll and Hyde children and this is quite common. Most of the time, the educators have the easiest role here, with the child being very well behaved and polite in their setting, but once they are at home, all hell breaks loose. We must listen to parents and carers and ask them what they see at home in terms of behaviour.

SUPPORTING CHILDREN'S EMOTIONS – A PRESCHOOL'S PERSPECTIVE

We spend time with the children in our setting, getting to know how they express their different emotions, helping them to express them verbally, and working out what makes them tick. This helps us to respond to different cues and to know if the child needs space or reassurance in order to help them to feel better. In our welcome pack, we ask parents to share their knowledge of their children, what upsets them and how to comfort them. We also spend time during circle time talking about different feelings with the help of a puppet turtle, Timmy, who is very shy. This provides an opportunity for the children to think about what makes them feel angry or sad, or happy or excited, and to discuss how this feels in their bodies, helping them to recognise their emotions. We also share these ideas with parents so they know what we are doing at preschool.

Research shows that the quality of the home learning environment (HLE) is more important for a child's development than parental occupation, education or income (Sylva et al., 2004). When thinking about what an effective HLE looks like, it comes down to simple things, for example, the amount of language used at home, sharing books and reading together, as well as undertaking activities such as visiting the library, drawing, painting and engaging in songs and nursery rhymes (National Literacy Trust & HM

Government, 2018). As educators we can support parents by offering them easy to implement ideas about things they can try at home and share information about our approach.

Building a relationship with parents in the first place is not always easy and should be one of our top priorities. It is our role, as educators, to build close, trusting and reciprocal relationships with parents and carers from the moment we are approached to care for their child. They have a lot to offer and can support us in planning what opportunities and experiences to offer their child next. It is important to remain non-judgemental when working with parents and carers. Parents have a difficult job and they haven't necessarily got the same levels of understanding about child development that we have. If we are able we can share our insights with them, focusing them around their child. Most parents are happy to talk about their children and enjoy hearing about what they do whilst in our care.

When it comes to assisting parents and carers with their child's behaviour, we need to avoid giving unwanted advice. It is better to ask if they would like any ideas to support their child and offer to share our thoughts, always being ready to talk if needed. One idea is to adopt a coaching approach, rather than a directive one. This is when we hold parents in positive regard and use open, creative questions to help them think more deeply about what they do and why in relation to their children's behaviour. Questions we might like to ask include:

- What their child could be communicating to us?
- What strategies have they already tried at home?
- What have they noticed works better at home?
- What could they do differently?
- Who could help?
- How can we strive for consistency between home and setting?

Many settings and schools arrange home visits before a child begins to attend so they can get to know the child in their own environment. Children usually feel safe at home and enjoy having their educator visit, often referring back to this, 'Remember when you came to my house…' Many educators have told me how beneficial they find these visits.

HOME VISITS – A PRESCHOOL'S PERSPECTIVE

Home visits before a child starts is one way of building the bond between parent and key worker. In my setting I find it is important that visits are mutually arranged to achieve maximum benefit for the child, and if this is not possible that there are other ways to build this relationship successfully. Conveying that you have an interest in a family and appreciate their ideas hopefully will empower them to work with you. To foster a positive relationship, educators must be friendly, open and non-judgemental.

We will also want to consider meeting the needs of parents/carers, for example do parents need an interpreter if English is not their first language or do they need help to understand the information? If possible, we need to provide opportunities for parents to see what goes on during a session, so perhaps a parent might like to spend time with us during the day. Many children will go home and simply say, 'I played', and having an open door policy and allowing parents in may help to give them an insight and offer them reassurance. Things were different during the various Covid restrictions, however we still needed to provide reassurance for parents that their children were well cared for and loved.

Consistency

Most behaviour books will talk about the importance of consistency when responding to children's behaviour. This is because as a general rule, children prefer predictable environments with a similar routine so they know where they stand, what the rules are and the expectations placed upon them. So we need to aim for consistency between home and our setting. Having a consistent approach also enables them to feel more safe and secure as mentioned in Chapter 1.

Ways that we can encourage consistency with home and within our setting include:

- Building positive relationships between staff and parents and carers.
- Getting to know our families individually.
- Sharing our approach to supporting behaviour.
- Encouraging the same rules both at home and in the setting.
- Ensuring all adults who look after the child have developmentally appropriate expectations for behaviour and respond in the same way.
- Sharing policies with everyone and ensuring that they are followed in terms of practice.
- Following through on any instructions or demands and being true to our word.
- Communicating effectively with staff and families.
- Sharing our children's next steps and achievements with parents and carers.
- Having a consistent routine.

ENSURING CONSISTENCY AT HOME – A NURSERY'S PERSPECTIVE

We support a girl who struggles, particularly at home. Her mother uses rewards regularly and gives them out for any reason, not just when the child is behaving in a way they want her to. Her father has lost the desire to engage and finds the little girl's behaviour difficult to manage at home. The nursery school has been talking to both parents to try to encourage more consistency of response between mum and dad.

Partnerships with others

Educators regularly work with other professionals as part of their day-to-day practice. Sometimes these may include stakeholders or people with a professional interest in the setting such as committee members, governors, managers or inspectors, whilst others may be involved because of specific children, such as social workers, health workers, area SENCos or inclusion officers. In addition to this we may work with members of the local community, charities, faith leaders and others. It is really important that we share our approach with these visitors so that everyone involved with the setting understands what we do and why we do things that way.

Here are four key principles that can help us when working with others:

1. Keep the child and our ethos at the centre and give the child a voice.
2. Ensure we communicate effectively with all and share any information accurately, gaining appropriate consents.
3. Build positive relationships based on mutual respect where we value all ideas and opinions.
4. Maintain professionalism by attending meetings, carrying out any actions we are given and remaining professional in our manner.

If we have any children with additional needs, we may find ourselves working with a range of others. Often we may have to attend discussions such as 'Team Around the Child' or other inclusion meetings. Our special educational needs and disabilities coordinator or equality named coordinator may need to be involved and it is important that we work together with parents and carers as well as others who may work with the child in the setting.

GLOBAL DEVELOPMENTAL DELAY – A SUPPORT WORKER'S PERSPECTIVE, RURAL PRESCHOOL

Working with Jordan reminded us there is always a reason for a child's behaviour. Jordan had been born prematurely and was under the care of a consultant paediatrician. The family had a complex range of medical and social needs and were receiving support from Home–Start. Jordan's parents took up an invitation for a home visit to discuss his needs and although they raised concerns about his behaviour, nothing major was noted initially when he started preschool. His start time was adjusted (earlier) to help him to settle in the mornings and we worked closely with the family and health visiting team. It became clear that Jordan was not meeting developmental milestones and referrals were made to Portage and Speech and Language Therapy (SALT).

Towards the end of Jordan's first term, he began biting and appeared to target one child in particular; the parents of this child raised a complaint. We supported both sets of parents through this challenging period as we understood there had to be a reason for the behaviour. Jordan's parents shared that he was biting at home as well. It seemed that incidents sometimes coincided with periods of separation when his parents were involved in hospital appointments and stays with siblings. Jordan's speech and language delay meant he was unable to communicate his needs and feelings. We felt that not only was he responding to periods of separation and stress, but he was also trying to instigate interactions with other children and did not know how to go about this. Eventually after many months a relationship blossomed between the two children. It prompted us to update our behaviour policy to include procedures for biting and to produce a leaflet which is given to both sets of parents affected by a biting incident.

Additional SEND funding paid for some support worker hours. While supporting Jordan, I worked closely with my manager and the Portage Worker. Collaboratively we produced Individual Plans which were reviewed fortnightly. Parents' input was welcomed, and I would regularly keep them updated on his progress or developmental areas in need of more intense support. Once a term we held *Team Around the Family* meetings attended by Jordan's parents and to which all professionals involved with the family were invited, e.g., Portage Worker, Home-Start, consultant paediatrician, SALT, Children's Centre family worker, Primary School SENCo and reception teacher. The family's dire housing situation was frequently discussed, and letters written to support a move. Jordan was sharing a bedroom with his parents and younger sibling. Neither parent was able to work, and Jordan's father became the carer for Jordan's mother. All of this was impacting the parents' mental health, and both were offered counselling, together with a parenting support course. Frequent hospital appointments and stays may have affected the maternal bond with Jordan, contributing to his separation anxiety and stress. Ways to re-establish the bond were suggested such as one-to-one time for Jordan with his mum.

I supported Jordan using a variety of methods and resources – including PEIC-D in play (a programme to help children develop their non-verbal communication skills), promoting positive behaviours through modelling and feedback, meaningful praise, sensory resources, narrative therapy, gross motor activities and small group play. When Jordan's mum went away for long periods, she recorded voice messages which he could listen to in preschool. I employed a total communication approach that included basic sign language, e.g., milk or water, alongside objects of reference as well as photographs. Given his speech delay, this enabled Jordan to understand and engage with the environment around him, and he was empowered to communicate his choices and needs. One resource which was beneficial was a Lego 'chewy' brick which Jordan wore like a necklace; this supported his need to bite and chew.

When we find ourselves engaging with other agencies or inter-professional working it is usually for the sake of a child, and whenever possible they should be given a voice. The UN Convention on the Rights of the Child is clear that the best interest of the child should always be a top priority (Article 3) and children should have their views taken into consideration about any decisions affecting them (Article 12) (UNICEF, 1989). The case study about Jordan demonstrates how settings can be successful in this as he was empowered to communicate through the total communication approach adopted. Chapter 5 has explored how we can authentically listen to children and ascertain their views.

Policy into practice

It is a good idea to have a written policy which outlines our approach to supporting children's behaviour. Many settings used to have a 'behaviour management' policy, however, as explained in Chapter 7, managing behaviour is not a term I like to use. Instead I prefer to say supporting children's behaviour. One setting I worked with has an 'Understanding and supporting children's behaviour policy', another has called their policy 'Promoting self-regulation through co-regulation and a loving pedagogy' which, as you can imagine, I was thrilled about!

Writing a policy is a useful exercise in itself because it requires us to really focus on what we do and why we do it that way. Policies help us to share our approach with others and be transparent about our practice. If we are able to, we can also involve children in writing our policy. Perhaps discussing our setting rules with them and talking about why we need to behave in certain ways and how we can be kind to our friends. Some settings include a few quotes from the children in their policies too. You may like to include the following in a policy:

- Policy statement. This is where we share what we believe about behaviour and why. So explain that all behaviour is communication and we need to understand and support children and acknowledge and validate their feelings.
- Our approach. This will include how we will respond to children in detail. It could include examples of 'When a child… Adults will…'
- The child's voice.
- How we work in partnership with parents and carers and the importance of this.
- A suggestion to read this in conjunction with our other policies.
- Ideas of where to access further information or support.
- When we will review this policy.

RELATIONSHIP MANAGEMENT POLICY – A PRIMARY HEADTEACHER'S PERSPECTIVE

Our primary school is reward and sanction free for many reasons. This does not mean unvalued and unrecognised; actually, it's the opposite. It means that we value an achievement for the effort it has taken at that stage in the process. It is personal recognition on a very individual level.

We completely understand wanting to praise and encourage children who are doing brilliant learning and are engaging with different activities, that doesn't have less impact if you do it privately and specifically. We understand the value of sharing it with others too – we all love a bit of positive feedback.

However, when we made the decision about ten years ago as a school not to 'reward', we asked the children about it. When asked

145

what they felt about our 'Star of the Week' awards, they replied, 'We know you like them!', 'We just know it is our turn!' or 'We know it isn't our turn!' When we asked what they needed when they had done something they were proud of, they told us they just needed someone whose opinion they valued to know about it and share that brilliant feeling in the moment. So that's what we do. All day, every day. It's personal. Surely every single member of our school community deserves celebrating, and their individual achievements, whatever they might be, noticing.

We understand that occasionally children will behave inappropriately for whatever reason. When children display this behaviour, there are several layers of consequences in place to encourage them to manage their behaviour in a positive way. As an educator we should always recognise 'all behaviour as communication' and ask what is the child trying to communicate to us? We realise that this is not the same for every child with their own packet of needs so it may look different in each individual case.

Our relationship policy is not primarily concerned with rule enforcement. It is a tool used to promote good relationships, so that people can work together with the common purpose of helping everyone learn. It uses restorative approaches which cover respect, taking responsibility, repair of relationships and reintegration. At our school we recognise the damaging effects of excluding children as it leaves them open to further social exclusion which increases the chance of future harm. As a result, we have a zero exclusion policy.

ACTIVITY

Write a letter to a parent explaining our current ethos in relation to supporting children's behaviour and emotions and how it underpins our policies and practice. Include a detailed description of our approach written in terms of 'When a child... Adults will...'

Concluding thoughts

Our ethos and the approach we adopt will have an impact on every aspect of our practice and should underpin everything we do in relation to how we support children's behaviour and emotions. Children and their social, emotional and mental health needs should be central to our provision and, I would suggest, adopting a loving pedagogy secures this in place. Building effective relationships with parents and carers and acknowledging their place as the child's first educator is a helpful place to start. When we work in true partnership it is easier to strive for consistency in our approach with home. We may also need to engage with other professionals in order to support specific children, and this chapter has outlined some key principles when working in this way with others. The next chapter draws together the themes of the book and summarises the key messages by considering the principles of nurture.

QUESTIONS FOR REFLECTION

How can we ensure consistency of response within our team?
How do we involve parents and carers in our setting?
How would we describe our ethos and approach in a nutshell?

Further reading

I have written several articles and blogs about developing a loving pedagogy. They can be found on my website at www.tamsingrimmer.com/copy-of-pedagogy-adult-s-roles
An interesting article about rewards: www.notimeforflashcards.com/2019/07/throw-away-the-sticker-charts-preschool-behavior-tips.html

References

Grimmer, T. (2021) *Developing a Loving Pedagogy in the Early Years: How Love Fits with Professional Practice.* London: Routledge.

Jung, I. and Smith, D. (2018) Tear down your behaviour chart. *Educational Leadership*, 76(1), 12–19.

Lungu, M. (2018) The influence of rewards used in child education over the development of their personality. *Journal Plus Education*, 19(1), 225–237.

National Literacy Trust & HM Government (2018) *Improving the Home Learning Environment: A Behaviour Change Approach.* Retrieved from www.gov.uk/government/publications/improving-the-home-learning-environment

Sylva, K., Melhuish, E., Sammons, P., Siraj-Blatchford, I. & Taggart, B. (2004) *The Effective Provision of Pre-School Education (EPPE) Project: Final Report: A Longitudinal Study Funded by the DfES 1997–2004* (Report). London: Institute of Education, University of London/Department for Education and Skills/Sure Start.

UNICEF (1989) United Nations Convention on the Rights of the Child. Available at www.unicef.org.uk/wp-content/uploads/2010/05/UNCRC_united_nations_convention_on_the_rights_of_the_child.pdf

Concluding remarks

How many times have you heard the cry, 'It's not fair!' Children have a real sense of justice, injustice, fairness and rules, regardless of whether or not they keep the rules themselves! I believe we should actively promote positive behaviour in our settings through the way we act, interact, speak and also through having developmentally appropriate expectations of children's behaviour.

In order to respond appropriately, we need to do everything we can to understand the child and the context in which they find themselves. Therefore, our observations are key. We need to get to know our children well, work out what motivates and fascinates them as well as what upsets and frustrates them. Then we can use this information to plan engaging, exciting and developmentally appropriate activities and there will be less time for challenging behaviour. We also need to work closely with parents and carers and try to establish some consistency between home and setting.

There are many ways that our daily practice can help to promote positive behaviour and support children emotionally. This book has introduced behaviour as communication and invited us to become behaviour detectives in order to better understand our children and be more accepting of their emotions. The key messages have been to recognise children's behaviour as communication, to acknowledge children's feelings and respond sensitively with understanding and empathy. Throughout the book I have shared many different strategies which I have described as tools in a toolbox, to be used as and when appropriate. It is my hope that through reading this book educators will better understand their children and feel more confident when responding.

DOI: 10.4324/9781003137474-11

Principles of nurture

We often use the term nurturing to describe our approach when working within early years. We mean it in the context of how we lovingly support children to develop in a certain way. When thinking about our behaviour, sometimes nurture is framed as opposed to nature, for example do children behave a certain way because it's innate and the way they naturally behave (nature) or it is down to the social environment they are growing within and its influence on them (nurture). Although often posed as a debate, nature versus nurture, I believe both to be partly responsible for the way we behave, with nurture perhaps taking more of the credit. So who you're with and the experiences you have in life will probably have more of an impact on your behaviour than your genes. We know the huge impact that trauma and adverse childhood experiences can have on children and that those who have a good start in life have significant advantages over those who, sadly, do not.

Within our early childhood settings we tend to adopt a nurturing approach where we recognise the impact and influence we can have on the children and act as co-regulators, helping them to become more resilient. This, in turn, raises their self-esteem and can contribute to higher levels of wellbeing. As I wrote this book I was reminded of the 'principles of nurture' (Lucas et al., 2006) and felt that they fitted in brilliantly with the themes, so I want to finish this book by outlining these principles.

The six principles of nurture should underpin our practice and will help children to achieve more in our schools and settings. They are:

1. Children's learning is understood developmentally.
2. The classroom/setting offers a safe base.
3. The importance of nurture for the development of wellbeing.
4. Language is a vital means of communication.
5. All behaviour is communication.
6. The importance of transition in children's lives.

(Lucas et al., 2006)

The first principle is about recognising the importance of having developmentally appropriate expectations and, as explained in Chapter 3, this will help nurture and promote children's wellbeing. It will also help us, as educators, to better understand our children and respond more appropriately. Having an understanding of child development is part and parcel of this.

Secondly, the principles make reference to attachment theory, stating that the classroom or setting should provide a safe base for our children from which they can explore and investigate. Chapter 1 thought about the importance of ensuring our children feel safe and secure and how adults have a key role to play in this.

The third principle is about the importance of nurturing relationships and how this promotes children's wellbeing. Chapter 1 also thinks about supporting children's wellbeing. One great way to do this is to use the Leuven Scale for Wellbeing and Involvement mentioned in Chapter 2 (Laevers, 2005). This scale has two parts, one that focuses on wellbeing and offers a five-point scale for assessing children's wellbeing, and the second which focuses on involvement and, again, offers a five-point scale for assessing how involved, or engaged, children are in their activity. I recommend finding out more about this free resource and using it in practice. There is a link to this scale in the additional reading and resources section at the end of this chapter.

Fourthly, this principle considers the importance of language as a vital means of communication. There are lots of different ways that we communicate – language is part of the story, but not the whole story. However, children who find language difficult to understand or who have trouble communicating will need additional support and nurture from us. The world can be a frightening place when we don't understand what's going on around us or we are unable to communicate our needs. We should consider the sort of language that we are using and how we can communicate more effectively in order to nurture our children. Chapters 4 and 6 think about using positive language, body language and sign language as well as using language to describe emotions in order to fully support children.

The fifth principle is the whole premise for this book, that is, all behaviour is communication. Every chapter continues with this theme and hopefully, in reading this far, the importance of viewing behaviour in this way is evident to all. We are to act as behaviour detectives trying to ascertain what children are communicating to us, so we can respond appropriately and proactively rather than reactively.

Lastly, the sixth principle highlights the importance of transition in children's lives and the impact change can have on them. Chapter 6 thinks about some strategies we can adopt which support children through change and transition and reminds us that we need to view our settings through our children's eyes in order to better understand what difficulties they may encounter.

Conclusion

Social, emotional and mental health (SEMH) needs could be described as children having difficulties in managing their emotions and behaviour. This is an area of growing interest as more and more educators become aware of the need to support children's mental health and wellbeing. Our behaviour is undeniably linked to our emotions and there is always a reason for children behaving the way they do. As educators we want to support our children emotionally and understand their behaviour. By viewing all behaviour as communication and using the many strategies outlined in this book, our children will be better supported, understood and feel safe and secure. If we use these ideas within a loving pedagogy it will be a powerful approach to adopt and one which children will hugely benefit from (Grimmer, 2021). The knock-on effect will be staff and children with high levels of wellbeing. What more could we want!

When I used to cry, 'It's not fair!' as a child, my Dad used to respond, 'Life's not fair!' which sounds a little harsh, however true it may be. But we need to acknowledge that for some children, life really isn't fair and we need to do everything in our power to change the world for these children. So let's remain positive and ensure that our settings are as fair as they can be, as we keep calm, carry on and support their behaviour and emotions.

It is really important to be a reflective educator and evaluate our practice regularly. This can sometimes be tricky to do honestly and can be unsettling because it can challenge what we do and question why we do it that way. Fook and Gardner believe that reflection is a 'process of unsettling individual assumptions' (2007, p. 16). Within an early childhood context, this could mean teaching new or innovative ideas, challenging mainstream viewpoints and contemplating our practice. Šaric and Šteh believe that moving outside an educator's comfort zone is necessary if deep critical reflection is to take place (2017). I have also found this to be true in my own practice, as reflecting upon my teaching, what my students or trainees are learning, and what I do in practice in the light of new research can be an uncomfortable process.

Despite it sometimes being unsettling or uncomfortable, it is vital that we reflect upon our role as an educator and ensure that we are improving our provision for the sake of the children. With this in mind I have gathered together several questions which I hope will enable educators to evaluate their practice. We need to answer these questions honestly, as a team, to review our practice, considering the perspective of all team members as valid and valuable. To gain a holistic view, we could also include the voice of the child, parents and carers, leadership team and any other stakeholders.

QUESTIONS FOR REFLECTION

Ethos:

- To what extent does our ethos and pedagogy reflect the six principles of nurture?
- Do we have a behaviour policy in place that accurately describes our practice? Can we review it in the light of our learning from this book?
- To what extent do our staff and children feel held in mind, noticed, valued, understood and missed if absent?
- How strong are our links with other settings and professionals? Do we know when and where to seek additional support?
- To what extent do we accept and validate all emotions for all people?
- Are we allowed to cry, laugh, 'stamp our feet' here? Are the children? And parents?
- Do we feel safe enough to admit mistakes in our setting and would we be forgiven?
- To what extent do we embrace difference and diversity and practice inclusion in relation to ability, identity, gender, culture, race and religion?

Enabling environment and routine:

- How does it feel to walk through our entrance doors? As a child, parent or member of staff?

- Consider how the setting feels from different perspectives – is it welcoming, loving and inclusive? What is it like to be in leadership in this setting? Or a cleaner? Or a parent-helper? Or a governor?
- How well does our provision meet the emotional needs of the children who attend?
- Have we planned for times during the day when children could find it difficult? e.g. transitions, arrivals, going home time, staff change-over etc.
- Have we considered the emotional environment of our setting?
- What opportunities are there in our routine to talk about feelings and emotions?
- Are there pictures or photographs of children experiencing different feelings and mirrors available to the children?
- How does our daily routine support children's independence and offer opportunities for calm?
- Do we have any calm areas and how are they used?
- Are sensory objects and materials freely available to the children (e.g. fiddle toys, squishies, blu-tac, poppets)?
- Do we have a range of multicultural activities and resources that reflect the background and culture of the children attending to help them feel safe and secure?

Role of the adult:

- Are adults trustworthy, reliable and consistent with the children in their care?
- Do all staff build warm, trusting relationships and show sensitivity to the needs and feelings of all other adults and children?
- Are staff aware of attachment and trauma issues and how best to support children in this area?
- Are adults positive role models, always displaying the behaviour we expect from children (e.g. using quiet voices, being respectful, resolving conflict, asking questions)?
- How do we maintain our own health and wellbeing and ensure that we remain emotionally regulated whilst maintaining and enhancing the wellbeing and emotional regulation of others?

- To what extent do adults use and promote emotion coaching and problem solving as a response to stress and conflicts?

Supporting the unique child:

- How well does our provision meet the individual needs of the children who attend?
- How do we ascertain the voice of the child?
- Do our children know that we love them and that they are very special? How do we know?
- To what extent do we explore and understand what children's behaviour is communicating to us?
- How do we continue to support children when their key person is away?
- Have we considered the use of transitional objects and comforters in our setting?
- Do we make assumptions or generalise for specific children (e.g. 'He's just a boisterous boy' or 'She is a biter')?
- Have we thought about the levels of wellbeing and involvement in our setting?

Parental engagement:

- How well do we know our parents, for example do parents feel able to share personal details with us such as changes at home?
- To what extent do we share our observations and documentation about children's attachments and behaviour with parents/carers?
- Have we considered parental separation anxiety and how we can support parents through this?
- Are we consistent when boundary setting in partnership with parents and across all age ranges?

In addition to these questions, at the end of every chapter there were three questions for reflection thinking about the theme in that chapter which can be considered alongside these.

Further reading

Additional resources

In addition to the books and resources recommended at the end of each chapter, the following may be of interest.

I have written several articles and blogs about many of the themes mentioned in this book. They can be found on my website at www .tamsingrimmer.com/articles

I also have some online training courses covering several of the themes in this book which can be accessed from the online courses tab of my website at www.tamsingrimmer.com/

An excellent online course on self-regulation: https://mineconkbayir .co.uk/online-programme/self-regulation-in-early-years/

SEMH

Mainstone-Cotton, S. (2017) *Promoting Young Children's Emotional Health and Wellbeing: A Practical Guide for Professionals and Parents.* London: Jessica Kingsley Publishers.

Mainstone-Cotton, S. (2021) *Supporting Children with Social, Emotional and Mental Health Needs in the Early Years: Practical Solutions and Strategies for Every Setting.* London: Routledge.

The Leuven Scales of Wellbeing and Involvement can be accessed at www.kindengezin.be/img/sics-ziko-manual.pdf

The Scottish Government have a range of resources to support wellbeing: www.gov.scot/publications/shanarri/

Schematic behaviour

Atherton, F. and Nutbrown, C. (2013) *Understanding Schemas and Young Children from Birth to Three.* London: Sage.

Athey, C. (2007) *Extending Thought in Young Children: A Parent–Teacher Partnership*, 2nd edn. London: Sage.

Louis, S., Beswick, C., Magraw, L. and Hayes, L. (2013) *Understanding Schemas in Young Children. Again! Again!* London: Bloomsbury.

Nutbrown, C. (2011) *Threads of Thinking*, 4th edn. London: Sage.

References

Fook, J. & Gardner, F. (2007) *Practising Critical Reflection* Maidenhead. London: McGraw-Hill Education.

Grimmer, T. (2021) *Developing a Loving Pedagogy in the Early Years: How Love Fits with Professional Practice*. London: Routledge.

Laevers, F. (2005) *Well-Being and Involvement in Care Settings: A Process-Oriented Self-Evaluation Instrument*. Leuven: Kind & Gezin and Research Centre for Experiential Education.

Lucas, S., Buckland, G. & Insley, K. (2006) *Nurture Group Principles and Curriculum Guidelines: Helping Children to Achieve*. London: Nurture Group Network.

Šaric, M. & Šteh, B. (2017) Critical reflection in the professional development of teachers: Challenges and possibilities. *Publication Center for Educational Policy Studies Journal*, 7(3) 67–86.

Index